DEDICATION

To my adventuresome spouse, Jack Schneider, who took me to live in South Africa; to my children, Karen Paff and Jonathan Longcore, who cheerfully read many stories as I worked on them; and to the memory of Elizabeth Mngadi, our Swazi flat cleaner in Johannesburg, who helped me adjust and keep a sense of humor while living under apartheid.

ACKNOWLEDGMENTS

This book could not have been written had my husband, Jack Schneider, not accepted a job in South Africa, and had Elizabeth Mngadi not been our flat cleaner. I am indebted to my assistant, Ana Nava, for keeping me and my writing organized despite all my clutter, and to Lee Blevins for his expertise with computers and cover design. And I sincerely thank the members of the Writer's Support Group, especially Carol Pechler and Chris Witzel, who edited countless drafts and guided me through the publishing process.

CONTENTS

SECTION I.

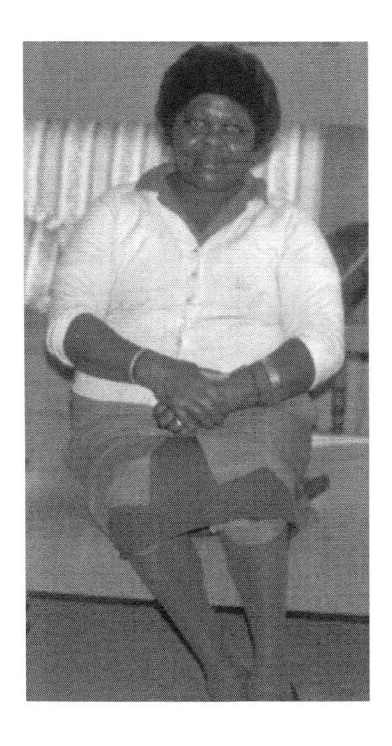

Elizabeth Mngadi © Elizabeth Schneider

MEETING ELIZABETH

The sharp, business-like knock on the door of our apartment implied no nonsense, so I responded quickly. Who could it be? The police…already?

But opening the door, I only saw two women: one, the manager, Mrs. Wood, a small, needle-thin white woman with dyed jet-black hair; and the other, a tall, ample black woman in a well-worn green uniform and knitted cap.

"Mrs. Schneidah, this is your flat cleaner, Elizabeth, who will do your floors and bawth Monday through Friday," Mrs. Wood said briskly, in a staccato British accent. "But don't ask her to do extras. She has seven other flats to clean," she warned.

I wasn't about to challenge Mrs. Wood on that point. I wondered if she was the person who had opened and read our mail this morning, then carelessly replaced it backward with no address showing through the windowed envelope, even though it was firmly sealed when I unlocked my mailbox.

"I'm glad to meet you, Elizabeth. I'm looking forward to your help," I said, smiling with relief as I reached out to shake her hand. This was an unexpected bonus that came with our rent.

"Yassum" was the only reply, no smile on her dark, round face. Ignoring my hand, she pulled herself erect, turned, then strode down the corridor, effectively projecting attitude.

"Elizabeth has been here for five years," confided Mrs. Wood, "and she's slow because she's so heavy. But she's honest and strong. I have a tedible time with many of the stawff here. They're always taking things, so keep your valuables locked up!"

"What's her last name?" I asked.

"I don't know her last name. I can't make out their crazy names. Why do you care? Ask to see her work permit. That'll tell you. They all have to carry work permits to show they have permission to come into Johannesburg."

"So where does she live?"

"She lives in Soweto, of course. They all live in Soweto, 15 miles away. They take the train in to Johannesburg in the morning, and then home to Soweto in the afternoon. The crowds are a mess down at the station about a mile from here, and it's veddy dangerous. Mugging goes on constantly, and sometimes my girls don't even get to carry their wages home at the end of the week. Those *tsotsis* crowd around and steal their money," she said with a sigh. "*Tsotsis*" were African street thugs armed with knives who prowl the streets, particularly on paydays.

"Because Elizabeth is big and only carries a plastic OK Bazaar grocery bag, she hasn't been mugged veddy often. She always wears a plain housedress and, of course, a knitted cap like they all do. Not a uniform like some of them, so the *tsotsis* don't think she has much money. I think she carries her work permit here," patting her bra. "Most of them do."

She sighed. I could see Mrs. Wood missed England.

"Oh dear, that must be a rough life," I said, beginning to realize that Johannesburg could be a dangerous place.

"But she's a hard worker, and even though she doesn't know much English, she's smart, kind of street savvy. So if you have trouble giving her directions, she'll probably figure it out." Mrs. Wood paused, adding "Well, good day," before leaving, her waning footsteps clicking "efficiency" in Morse code as she crisply walked down the corridor.

Elizabeth appeared to be about my age, 53, and I looked forward to getting to know her and finding out more about life for the black people in this apartheid world of South Africa. I realized that would not be easy in this firmly segregated country.

I heard her key in the door the first day she came and noted she was right on time. I was impressed at how diligently she worked. She cleaned the floors and used her broom under the stove and the bed. She didn't try to engage in chitchat, did her work efficiently and then left. She was brusque enough that I was puzzled. I suspected that Mrs. Wood had warned her against getting chummy with any of the residents. Getting to know Elizabeth would be a challenge, but because she came every weekday, I might be able to get to know her better over morning tea.

FLYING TO SOUTH AFRICA

Sitting in the plane to Johannesburg in 1975, I thought about my first impression of South Africa when we had visited by car four years earlier. On our Mozambique side there were two simple toilet sheds labeled "Men" and "Women" in Portuguese. Thirty yards into South Africa, I saw in sharp contrast, six sheds. Those were labeled, in English, "White Men," "White Women," "Coloured Men," "Coloured Women," and finally "Black Men" and "Black Women." The difference was so striking that I had taken several photographs.

I looked down upon the unusual geographical landscape of South Africa feeling deep misgivings. This country was to be our new home. Jack had accepted a tenured Lectureship in Mathematics at the University of Witwatersrand, a famously liberal, English-speaking university with about 15,000 students: white, black and coloured.

"Jack," I said worriedly, "are we ready for this?"

"Now you tell me! Remember, if it's intolerable, we can always leave," Jack responded with irritation, but his face showed concern as well.

Some of our American friends, referring to South Africa as an outcast or pariah, had forcefully assured us they would never visit us in "a country that legally practices apartheid." "Apartheid" means, literally "separateness" and more explicitly, "racial separation" in Afrikaans, the language of the Afrikaners, descendants of Dutch immigrants who settled in South Africa beginning in the 15th century.

Apartheid appalled us as well, but if you were going to help change things in a country and get to know and educate the blacks as well as the whites, we believed it was more realistic to accept that being *in* the scene would be more helpful than being *out* of it.

And I had my own private agenda, which was to register at

the university and earn my Ph.D. in African art.

What could we possibly do to help the blacks get educated when this entire country seemed to be against the idea? And how could we even get to know any blacks?

As the Lufthansa plane slowly turned inland from the turquoise Indian Ocean, it flew over the steep, rocky Drakensburg (Dragon's Teeth Mountain) range separating the lowlands from the bushveld. I had noted that Durban and Kwa-Zulu on the coastal green lowlands looked steamy-hot and lush with many palm trees.

In contrast, the next higher elevation, called the bushveld, was sparse, brownish-gray with scrub trees and willows mixed in with the swaying palms. It too, I was told, was rife with malarial mosquitoes and ticks like the lowlands, causing fevers and illnesses that spawn special hospitals with doctors knowledgeable about tropical diseases.

The plane glided on toward the highveld, a tan, desert-like plain more than a mile high that had no native trees taller than 15 feet. Before our landing on that unexpectedly high plain, one could see the different contours of the three South African ecological areas, lowland, bushveld and highveld, looking like an enormous upside-down saucer in Africa's blazingly bright sunshine.

In the center of the highveld lay the vibrant, pulsing city Johannesburg. "Joburg," as the whites called it, the economic hub, the business center and the largest, most important city in South Africa. This intense, noisy metropolis was surrounded by high mounds of dull yellow mine tailings planted with grasses to keep the dust down, although they usually didn't. The dross came from the myriad gold mines opened around 1849, about the same time as our gold rush in California. Joburg, or "i-Goli" as the blacks called it, referred to these innumerable mines, some more than a mile deep. (In Zulu, the small prefix "i" was always attached to a borrowed foreign word, in this case, "Goli" for gold.)

Up until 1994, when the massive majority of all races

voted in the first truly democratic election, there were three different capitals in the country: the Administrative Capital in the conservative city of Pretoria, the Judicial Capital in the even more conservative city of Bloemfontein, south of Johannesburg, and the Legislative Capital in the very British Cape Town at the southern tip of Africa. How strange for a country to have three different capitals!

Flying from California to South Africa was exhausting. First, there was a 12-hour flight to Germany. From there we had to transfer planes after an overnight layover, and then take another 12-hour flight to Johannesburg. With all of this, plus a time difference of 10 hours and a huge altitude difference (Johannesburg is more than a mile high), by the time we arrived, I felt like a zombie. I was so numb from all the work I had done in clearing our house and packing, I hadn't thought about what my impressions would be when arriving in South Africa as an immigrant.

We didn't like that category, but Jack's new job required it. We had nervously researched and found that our immigrant status would not affect our American citizenship. And, fortunately, it could be changed when leaving South Africa. That information had made the status bearable, but we were still uncomfortable.

Arriving at the Johannesburg airport, we found to our embarrassment that as immigrants we had privileged status entering the country. We were treated with special care because we were both white and new immigrants. We found out later that the South African government also gave generous tax advantages to white families for having babies. The government felt it was important to increase the white population.

The tall, blond and handsome Afrikaner immigration agents treated us extremely well as they triumphantly paraded us in front of the few tourists in a queue waiting to legally enter South Africa. They seemed to be saying, "See, these are Americans who want to live in our country" as they proudly and ostentatiously led us to our special, short queue.

Passport Control was so eager to have us come in that they greased all the wheels. By this time I was thoroughly upset by the situation, and, privately, I thoroughly hated each and every one of those tall, blond and handsome Afrikaner immigration agents.

We finished signing all of the official papers and hailed a black taxi driver to take us into the city to begin our new life in this curiously strange and beautiful country.

The government had made it easy and welcoming for us to get *into* South Africa, but could we get out again?

BISCUITS AND PHOTOS

Here in South Africa, everyone stopped for "elevenses," tea at 11 a.m. Elizabeth and I began to do the same, although I had to bribe her into having tea with me by offers of special biscuits (cookies). She really preferred having her tea upstairs with her cleaning friends, but I finally was able to lure her into having tea with me after several weeks by offering a new and different biscuit each time.

Elizabeth Mngadi was a cheery, ample woman about 53 years old. She didn't really know her age. The Swazi didn't keep birth records when she was born. She was the typical height of a black woman, perhaps 5'4" – but heavier than most women. It seemed to me she must have weighed over 200 pounds, or roughly 14 stone, the British 14-pound unit of measure used by English-speaking South Africans. She was completely comfortable with her shape, which was round: round face, round eyes, round belly, round bosom. Like all female black workers, she always wore a hat covering her head. She wore her knitted tam o'shanter like a halo above her moon-like face.

Eventually I learned that her husband had died of pneumonia from mine dust in his lungs. She was supporting her seven children and her mother, plus her deceased uncle's four children. Her mother lived nearby, but everyone else lived together in the uncle's house. Elizabeth spoke Zulu and a smattering of Afrikaans. Her English was limited and my Zulu non-existent, but communication can be deeper than that.

I also wanted to get to know more of the other black people who made our block of flats function. As time went on, I devised a way to get to know a few. I let word out, through Elizabeth, that I had a camera and would be happy to take pictures and give them to anyone who wanted to have their picture taken. All they had to do was come to Flat 701. We had to be discreet. If Mrs. Wood, the live-in manager, knew what I was doing, she would throw us out for being anti-apartheid troublemakers. I had already noticed the building had separate lifts, one labeled "Residents" for whites and the other labeled "Staff" for the blacks.

My photo project started slowly. Peter, the furnace man, arrived and asked that I take a picture of him with his most prized possession, his boom box radio. That was easily done, as he posed on the small, round cowhide rug in the center of the room, his hand lovingly placed on his boom box.

Over the next couple of weeks, more people arrived. Josiah, the night watchman, brought his wife from Soweto carrying their new baby. They posed self-consciously on our rug. The success of this charming picture was assured.

Another employee had, remarkably, brought in a tall electric stand lamp from Soweto, which must have been difficult to carry on the crowded train. Most of Soweto was not wired for electricity, but, under pressure, the government was gradually installing electric power in certain areas. Evidently this man was proud that his home had electricity, and wanted a photo to prove it.

"Would you like to have your picture taken, too?" I asked Elizabeth, who had seen some of these sessions with growing interest. "Nope," she shook her head firmly.

I had noticed that after a few days of working for us, she began doing little things in the kitchen to catch my eye. Our dingy aluminum teakettle began to sparkle after Elizabeth found the scouring pads and polished it mirror-bright each day. She attacked my aluminum soup pot, rubbing it until it gleamed. She seemed in less of a hurry to hustle out to her next flat and would help me make the bed. As I carelessly pulled up the sheets, she would carefully pick up the pillows, holding them by one corner, then the center, and shake them vigorously. She then carefully smoothed the bed after it was made. I was impressed.

So impressed that, when she broached the idea that I should hire her extra to do the laundry and ironing, I was tempted, despite Mrs. Wood. However, as Americans who never ironed, wearing only knit or wrinkle-proof clothes, I didn't really leap at the chance. I didn't want Jack to become accustomed to freshly ironed shirts that I would never continue doing. But sheets and towels? That was a real temptation.

"Wash? But how?" I asked her. "We've no machine and the laundromat is far away,"

"Tub" she said, amused by my ignorance.

"How would you rub out spots?"

"Board" she explained patiently, scrubbing in pantomime with her hand.

Sure enough, after I had succumbed to her alluring laundry suggestion, Elizabeth appeared the following day with an old plank that she propped up in the bathtub. After that, on her knees next to the bathtub, she did our weekly laundry in the morning before cleaning the flat, and then hung it out on the balcony to dry. At the end of her workday, she returned to bring in the dry wash. Next day she ironed it all.

The ironing appalled me, however, because with her very hot iron our clothes would never again be wrinkle-proof and would need to be ironed from then on. But they certainly were crisp and professional looking. We'd never looked so elegant and "smaht" (as they say in South Africa). We were doomed to be well dressed as long as Elizabeth took care of our clothes.

REFRIGERATOR SHOPPING

"When are you getting a refrigerator?" Jack asked impatiently. "Fortunately we've been invited to the da Silvas' for dinner tomorrow night, but don't you think you should get this flat into working order?"

Our unspoken division of labor implied this was my job. I knew I had to start purchasing furniture for our small flat near the university, but had postponed it while exploring some of the more interesting possibilities I might pursue during this new life in South Africa. But Jack was right. I needed to finish the job.

The kitchen already had a stove, but the small, leaking icebox left by the previous tenant wasn't something I wanted to live with. It was time to replace it with a real refrigerator, even though appliances here cost double the price in the states. It would have to be small, about the height of my navel I figured, eyeing the available space under the counter. But I had adjusted to that since every refrigerator we had owned since living overseas had never been any higher. I had discovered I could fit a liter milk bottle into the shelf in the door.

"Look at this ad, Jack. It says here they're having a sale on appliances, and they're offering one small refrigerator, special sale, at 350 rand!"

"That's about $450 today. Umm, okay, though it costs triple what we would pay in the States for it."

"I'll go down early in the morning before the crowd and see if I can get it."

"Do you know where the store's located?" he asked.

"Well, it says downtown Johannesburg, so I'll just drive into town, buy the fridge and get home early, about the time you'll be finished with your classes."

The appliance store was scheduled to open at 9 a.m., so I arrived at 8:15 thinking I would be first in line. I drove past the store to get oriented before parking and was surprised to see about 30 people had already lined up, waiting for the doors to open. By the time I had parked and walked back to the store, the queue had increased to almost 40 people, mostly black.

We all need to find bargains, I thought, and joined them at the end of the line. I pulled out my small notebook to make some notes while waiting. The other people seemed friendly with each other, talking back and forth, but since it was mostly in Zulu and Sotho I couldn't join in the conversation. It seemed like a congenial neighborhood gathering, and I enjoyed being part of the scene. The day was bright and sunny, pleasantly warm despite our mile-high altitude.

Time passed slowly, and the line of people near the doorway in front of the store's large plate glass windows increased as opening time approached. About 10 minutes before the doors were to be opened, two yellow armored police conveyances (called "caspirs") pulled up, filled with policemen. I wondered what this was all about, noting the policemen were all black.

With a shout, several policemen leaped down, and then, opening the rear doors of both caspirs, they released five or six large snarling dogs, German shepherds and a Doberman, that promptly set upon those of us waiting in line.

I was shocked, paralyzed with fear. What was going on? Thinking this was all a terrible mistake, I shouted to the black man behind me, through the din of growling dogs, screaming shoppers and yelling police, "What's happening?"

"Run, get outta here!" he shouted back in English. "Get into a store!"

I wasn't sure my wobbly legs would move. They had become like rubber. But one of the dogs, wildly barking and slobbering through his teeth, charged the black woman in front of me. Then he whirled, snapping at my ankles. I fled in the other direction. Next door was a furniture store, where the watching owner held the door open so I could safely escape inside, along with several other people, including the black woman. The door closed and we were safe, but I was shaking and breathing hard, close to tears.

I collapsed into a chair the owner brought for me, but could hardly speak. The whole event had happened so fast and was so incomprehensible to me that I couldn't find any words that would fit. Yes, I knew that this could be a violent country, but I thought the violence was between white and black. So why would black policemen attack innocent black shoppers? In fact, why would any of us peacefully waiting for an appliance store to open attract the police and their dogs?

After a few minutes and a glass of water, I weakly asked the storeowner, "Why? Why did the police do this? What were we doing wrong?"

"Why? This happens often here in downtown Joburg when there's an attractive sale going on. The store owners are worried that the crowd waiting to get into the sale will stampede when the doors open, and their large glass windows will be broken. It's happened before."

"Stampede? Everyone was quietly waiting in line until the dogs were let loose," I said.

"I know, but sometimes even if the store owners don't call the police, the police will see lots of people gathered in a crowd before a store's big sale, and if it looks dangerous, they'll set their dogs on them or use fire hoses to disperse them. It's a safety measure these days."

"But these were black police," I said. "Somehow I thought all the police in South Africa were white, not black."

The black woman shopper who had escaped with me turned and laughed bitterly. "The black police are the worst!"

The white storeowner nodded soberly. "They relish their role. It's one place they can show their power. It's best to avoid all police at any time."

By now the police had dispersed the crowd, and several policemen were attaching leashes to their dogs. As they herded the animals back into the caspirs, one of the drivers started his engine to leave. The other yellow caspir stayed there until the doors of the appliance store officially opened at 9 a.m., as had been advertised.

"I guess we can leave now," said the black woman who had escaped the melee when I did. "Thanks for letting us in," she added, turning to the white storeowner.

"Any time," the owner said, sincerely.

As I slowly recovered from my terror, I too, thanked the owner and left. Still feeling weak, I walked the few streets back to my car. My purchase of a new refrigerator had better be postponed until I learned more about shopping in Johannesburg.

At our elegant dinner that night at architect da Silva's home, I told them what had happened.

"You should never shop in downtown Johannesburg" Marta, his wife, said calmly. "It has become too dangerous."

"Well then, where do you shop when you have to get a refrigerator?" I asked.

"You go to one of the white suburbs like Rosebank or Sandton. That's where everyone we know shops."

We had known the da Silvas since the time we had all lived in Mozambique, three years before, and I had met many of my black friends at dinners in their home. They were liberal people, politically, and I expected them to share my horror, but they seemed quite matter of fact about today's incident.

It was incredible to me. Had they changed? True, they had left the country for Johannesburg when Mozambique's violent independence revolution spread to the capital where they lived. Marta still had South African citizenship. But Armando was Portuguese, and they had been happily living in Mozambique for 30 years.

How could such cosmopolitan people accept living here? I thought. *How could anyone? What would we be like if we stayed several years?*

GETTING ORIENTED

As Elizabeth and I were having tea and biscuits one morning, I realized adjusting to apartheid in South Africa would take longer than I had expected. For example, I wanted to know more about where Elizabeth lived and to understand her life. What had originally intrigued me about her was that she happened to have my name and was about my age. But after her coming to our flat each weekday morning and sharing our morning tea together, I was looking forward to the opportunity to know her better.

"Where do you live in Soweto?" I asked her.

The name "Soweto" is a contraction of the original term "South West Township." Soweto is an enormous satellite city 15 miles outside Johannesburg. It is composed of several million black people from separate tribal groups that speak different languages. Language was the organizing principle the Nationalist Government used to separate the different tribal sections in Soweto.

"Where do I live in Soweto?" asked Elizabeth repeating my question, "Jabulani, an' I take the train to Joburg ever' day. The ticket, she costs me lotsa money," she added.

"What does the name 'Jabulani' mean in Zulu?" I asked.

"It mean 'heppiness,' I'se heppy," she explained, using her ample body to demonstrate the meaning with a little dance step.

There are different districts in Soweto, just as in any large city. Each has a flavor based on several things: a resident's income (which is related to the size of the lot, or stand) and whether the stand has its own running water (or tap) outside the house in the back. Some houses only have a neighborhood tap used by several families. The other marker is the type of outhouse, whether or not it has a flushing toilet.

The dominant African language that is spoken creates another neighborhood flavor. The Sotho speakers live in one area, the Zulu speakers (and Swazi since it is similar) in another, the Shangaan from Mozambique speakers in a third, but the few Venda speakers are combined with other minority groups such as the South Sotho speakers. Part of the reason is the language of instruction in the school. If the school has Zulu-speaking teachers, communication is much easier for the children who come from homes where Zulu is the home language.

According to the government, the official population of Soweto was less than a million. By using that lesser figure, they hoped to avoid criticism from other countries over their apartheid policy. The government ignored the fact that many of the people in Soweto have extended families that include their live-in, rural relatives. These relatives can say they live in Soweto and therefore can work in Johannesburg. However, if their residence permit says they are from, for example, Jacob Botha's farm, Middelburg, by law they wouldn't be able to work in Johannesburg.

Population control—both controlling where the races lived and encouraging growth of the white population -- was a vital part of the apartheid government beginning with the Nationalist Party's emergence in 1948. Another reason rural families lived with relatives in Soweto is that by living there, their children could go to school in Soweto instead of the usually inadequate farm and mission schools. (Later, in those turbulent days of the 1970s and '80s, there was often a reverse trend of Soweto children going to live with a relative in the country where there was far less violence.)

A farm school was one that the farmer had organized on his property, so that the tenant workers living on his farm would have a place to send their children. The farmer and his neighbors paid for the teacher. These one-room schools varied widely in their educational quality and goals, and the highest grade was usually Standard Two, the equivalent of American fourth grade. Many of the domestic workers and rural women I had talked to had minimal education. Finishing the fourth grade seemed to be the norm, but many rural women had no education at all. Out of the 200 women I eventually interviewed in my fieldwork, which included 175 rural and 25 township women, the highest grade achieved was that of one Sowetan woman who had finished high school.

The problems for the blacks were great. When farmers needed more hands to work on the farm, they hired poorly paid tenants. Tenants were expected to build their own shelters from twigs and mud. In addition, blacks generally had the attitude that education should be for the boy, not the girl. "A girl can always work as a domestic worker without education," they said. Elizabeth, for example, a true city child, had only finished the second grade in Zulu (not as high as Standard Two) and was proud of having accomplished that much.

Another problem for the blacks was the language of instruction, which was one of the main triggers for the Soweto riots in 1976. The black students had rebelled at being taught in Afrikaans. They felt speaking Afrikaans was not as useful as English in the world. Many also felt Afrikaans was the language of the oppressors who had put into place the original apartheid system when the Nationalist Party came into power in 1948.

Of course that was an over-simplification of the problem. The British people actually had been fairly content for a long time with the separation of races. They profited by having low wage earners working in the mines. Eventually the British began to develop more conscience about it and tried in many ways to make the system more equal.

The few blacks living in Johannesburg were live-in maids working for wealthy white families. They usually lived in a small separate building in back of the family's big house.

White families referred to their servants as "the staff,"

which often consisted of a maid, cook, guard, gardener-and-driver, and sometimes a butler. There could be more than one of each, depending on the size of the house and garden and how much entertaining the homeowners did. Of course, there were less wealthy white people who had someone come in from Soweto to do the work required to keep their homes running smoothly.

The servants usually wore uniforms, but occasionally wore ordinary work clothes. In Elizabeth's case, she was part of a cleaning crew that worked for the owners of the Bridgeport flats, and these women all lived in Soweto. The building owners supplied their uniforms, which the women could take home to wash. Elizabeth wore an aged, shabby green uniform that had belonged to another heavy-set cleaning woman.

The male staff in our building lived in the servant's quarters on the 11th floor. Therefore, they were available whenever needed. They included the building watchman, Josiah, and the furnace man, Peter. Josiah had a handsome uniform with brass buttons that had been provided by the building owners. A building watchman's appearance gave outsiders a clue as to how protected a building was and perhaps an idea of the rental cost. Peter, the furnace man, wore his old clothes when he worked, but few people outside of the residents saw Peter unless he was substituting for night watchman duties.

In Bridgeport, the thin, energetic manager, Mrs. Wood, did an efficient job of keeping the whole building running smoothly. One time we held a dinner party for faculty in Jack's Maths and Computer Science Department. The guests included two professors from India who had brought their wives.

Mrs. Wood evidently heard about it, because just as one of the Indian men was performing an original composition on the sitar with his wife singing, there was a sharp rap on our door. When I opened the door, Mrs. Wood announced loudly, "I understand you have some 'coolies' in there, and that is not permitted in this building," much to my embarrassment. I wasn't sure who she meant by 'coolies,' but felt it wasn't complimentary.

Jack, hearing Mrs. Wood's voice, came to the door to see what the problem was. I explained, and he quickly stepped outside and closed the door so others wouldn't overhear the conversation.

He said, controlling his rage, "We're having a dinner party for the university's Maths Department. What is your problem?"

"You have some 'coolies' in there, and that is not permitted here in this building," Mrs. Wood repeated firmly.

Jack, realizing she was referring to our Indian guests, responded, "If that is the case, we are moving out tomorrow. Furthermore, I intend to call the owners of the building and see if that actually *is* one of the rules here."

We then returned inside, and he closed the door firmly. Fortunately, our Indian friends had not heard the conversation, so our party continued.

When Jack called the flat owners the next day, they were properly embarrassed and, knowing we were Americans, hastily assured us, "Mrs. Wood, unfortunately, is one of the old school Brits, and we will remind her that our policy here is that anyone came come, as a visitor, to any resident's flat."

So we continued to stay in Bridgeport and did our best to avoid Mrs. Wood.

HOME SECURITY

As I made my way to Margaret and Raymond Jaffe's house for afternoon tea in the wealthy northern suburbs of Johannesburg, the substantial size of the homes amazed me. Not that you could see them clearly. They were all surrounded by 12-foot concrete walls topped with broken glass plus a roll of razor wire above that. Razor wire is a variation of barbed wire, but instead of barbs made of knotted, pointed wires every few feet, small razor blades are spaced along the wire. Vicious razor wire seemed to me going beyond the necessary, but then we hadn't lived in Johannesburg that long. The heavy, locked gate with an embedded camera and speaker ensured that outsiders could not get in without scrutiny.

Several metal signs on the outside wall had printed warnings announcing "Armed Response" in large letters. I was later told that meant the hired security company, when triggered, took their responsibility seriously and would arrive with guns drawn. Obviously one didn't casually drop in at a friend's house, day or night, without calling first. Evidently the only way to get into a person's home in this wealthy suburb was to make your appointments ahead so your friend would be expecting you. Then the owner could use the camera and speaker at the gate to verify who you were and instruct one of the maids or the gardener to let you in.

This turned out to be the routine I had to go through to let Margaret know I had arrived, even though she knew I would be coming for tea at 3 p.m. The maid accordingly let me in, and Margaret met me at the door.

"How nice you could come. My friend Millicent said you and your husband would be here for a few years and to be sure to invite you for tea. You're very welcome to our home."

I thought warmly of Millicent, our mutual friend now living in New York. Millicent, a middle-aged South African, and her husband, formerly a wealthy entrepreneur in Johannesburg, had decided that South Africa was becoming too unstable for them to spend their declining years here, so they had emigrated to the States.

Thus, Millicent and her husband made yearly trips from New York back to South Africa to use their South African money or convert it to something of value that was portable and permitted in the States. Currency was carefully controlled in both countries, and passports were stamped inside with all the legal information about relevant currency laws. The yearly travel for Millicent and her husband was tedious, but they enjoyed coming back to Johannesburg to see their friends. During these visits they were able to gradually transform their South African wealth into objects they could legally bring into the United States. Her two new fur coats, their new Mercedes and the money from selling their magnificent home were all ways to dismantle their wealth.

In New York, Millicent had given me a list of names of some of her South African friends whom we should look up. Margaret and Raymond Jaffe were two of them, but we had not had time to get in touch with the others.

Millicent, presently in Johannesburg to visit her South African friends, asked them if I had gotten in touch. She was not happy that I hadn't. She called me on the phone and abruptly said, "Betty, I gave you a list of my wonderful friends here that I wanted you to get to know, but everyone I've contacted here tells me they've never heard from you."

I made weak excuses: "Getting settled, getting enrolled at the university" and a few other limp alibis.

It wasn't deliberate. We really had had a difficult time finding an appropriate place to live before we finally chose the Bridgeport flats. Somehow, American style, I had assumed buying a house would be the most economical way to live since we would be in South Africa for several years.

After I finally had found a house appropriate for Jack and me and enthusiastically told him about it, he looked at me in exasperation, saying,

"You have a house in California. Why do you want *another* house in South Africa? Isn't one house enough for you? Think of roof repairs; think of the security here which we know nothing about. Are you really sure you want to own a house here?"

Presented to me in this matter-of-fact way, I realized that, no, I didn't want to own another house. By then I was becoming aware of the security problems of living in a house here. A day and a night watchman working in a block of flats, plus other security protections such as living on an upper floor and having a monitored lift to take us safely up to it, suddenly made a simple flat sound much more attractive than a house.

"But paying a monthly rent, with nothing to show for it?" I timidly asked, trustingly bringing my old-world American economics into this new-world country.

"A flat would be far less of a problem than having to arrange furniture for a house, garage for the car, a watchman, and who knows what else," he said, sensibly.

So we had moved into Bridgeport, a building of flats located within easy walking distance to the university, only six blocks. Braamfontein was not an elegant neighborhood, more of a small business area, but close to our University of Witwatersrand. We furnished the flat with various pieces of furniture that the outgoing South Africans and foreigners were selling at bargain rates so that they could leave the country with some money.

We had settled into our flat, established our university connections, and I had enrolled as a post-graduate student for a Ph.D., with an advisor in the Social Anthropology Department, the very-British Professor Hammond-Tooke.

At long last, I looked at the list of her friends that

Millicent Rothschild had given me before our arrival in Johannesburg. I called the first names on the list, Margaret and Raymond Jaffe. Margaret had invited me over for tea, in true British fashion. I was curious to meet Raymond, since his sister was the only female Member of Parliament and known worldwide to be staunchly against apartheid. It was a connection I was looking forward to making.

Thus, this day, almost a year after we had arrived, I was beginning to follow up on the list of names that Millicent had given me long ago. Finally the day had arrived.

"Let's have our tea in the living room," Margaret suggested, as we left the spacious entry hall and headed for the living room.

"Beauty," she called to her longtime maid (whose looks didn't really fit her name), "Serve us our tea in the living room, please."

We turned toward the living room, but she found the living room door was locked.

"Oh dear," Margaret said, slightly irritated. "I've forgotten to unlock it since last night."

"You lock your living room door at night?" I asked, puzzled.

"Oh my, yes," she replied. "We lock up the living room because of our Oriental rugs, which we don't want stolen in case the house is burgled. We also lock our bedroom door at night for safety. We have night watchmen walking in the neighborhood each night as well.

"You'll get used to the security we all have to use these days. You've been here such a short time…" her voice trailed off.

She brought out her heavy ring of keys and unlocked the living room door so we could go in and sit down. It was a lovely big room with two large Oriental carpets on the floor. We sat facing each other on elegant upholstered chairs with the tea table between us.

When Beauty came in carrying the heavy silver tray with

the silver teapot and its matching cream and sugar containers, I looked with anticipation to see what variety of biscuits would be served. I remembered Elizabeth's similar reaction when I served tea in our flat. But Margaret didn't serve packaged shortbread biscuits as I did. She had selected elegant deli-sweets for our tea.

"Cheers, you're here," said Margaret, lifting her delicate teacup.

"Cheers, and I'm looking forward to knowing you better," I responded, little knowing how well I would get to know her, and especially her husband Raymond, a Queen's Counsel.

STUDENT PARADE

A few weeks into our new flat in Johannesburg, I heard the playful brass band of Wits University marching up Jorisson, the street that connected our block of flats with the university six blocks away.

It was the main street, the heart of our community, Braamfontein. Horns tooted, student drum majorettes in colorful short skirts twirled batons in unison. The majordomo in his smart white uniform led them crisply, thrusting his long staff up and down with the beat. Following the band was a very tall student, several heads higher than the rest, who cleverly marched on stilts hidden by his long pants. Students sat and hung onto open cars shouting, "Get your Wits Rag now," while waving the university's annual humor magazine over their heads to sell to the public.

More laughing students marched in groups, and you could see their exuberance at having finished their Wits Rag, now for sale. Pedestrians cheerfully handed over their rand because everyone knew the profits were going to needy black charities. Liberal Wits had long held a reputation for community service and social justice.

Elizabeth, Joyce and a number of other cleaning staff quickly clustered on Bridgeport's open roof terrace on the 11th floor, cheering the students on. "Look at the man with the long legs" shouted Elizabeth, pointing to the student on stilts, "and the gulls in their shiny skurts and whirling sticks! Woo-oo-oo!" Her eyes were big and her round face beamed. Her knit hat seemed a corona around her head.

"Lissen to the music," cried Joyce as the women leaned over the railing, full of enthusiasm for the parade. They loudly clapped and ululated to show their delight.

THE ENGLISH VS. AFRIKANERS

One of my first shocks in adjusting to life in South Africa was realizing the enormous chasm between the white people, that is, between the Afrikaans-speaking whites and the English-speaking whites. It seemed the Boer War that had raged at the turn of the century was still going on. There was much competition as well as lack of communication between the white students on both sides.

For whites, there were many private schools at the elementary and secondary level, and they were all firmly divided down language lines. There was very little interaction between them. These students seldom knew each other, even when they lived in the same area. If you grew up in an Afrikaans family, that was your language, that was your school, those were your friends, and those were whom you dated. Even universities were separate—four for English speakers and many more for Afrikaans students.

I remember one evening when, as faculty members of the English-speaking University of Witwatersrand (Wits), we were asked to chaperone a social function being held with the Afrikaans-speaking Rand Afrikaans University (RAU) students to discuss common university experiences. The administration hoped that RAU, the large, well-endowed Afrikaans university located only a few miles from us, and Wits, somewhat less endowed, would have an opportunity to socialize.

Despite these two groups of dating-age teens having grown up in Johannesburg, a mid-sized city, few of them had ever met members of the other language group. Fortunately some of the Afrikaans students prided themselves on knowing English as well as Afrikaans, so they could communicate. Our Wits students, even the few who knew Afrikaans, were reluctant to use the language and were happy to stay in English for the discussion.

More than that, what startled me was that here were two groups of young people in their late teens who had never had contact with each other because of different languages. Or if they had, it was very brief. Talk about the lack of contact and communication between black and white! Here the chasm was between whites and almost as great.

FILMING IN SOWETO

We had been in Johannesburg several months when I got hired onto a film crew one day. I was at my desk sorting proof sheets of pictures taken a few days before, when we did a segment at Orlando High School in Soweto. The footage was to be part of the background for our United Nations Habitat film "Housing in Southern Africa." It was my first visit to the black township.

"Soweto! You're going to Soweto?" Elizabeth had asked incredulously.

The curious Sowetan students of Orlando High School were lively but rather rough when a group of them eagerly charged up to our van wanting to see the cameras and tripods and to find out why four white people were coming into their black community. South African black students were not sorted into classes by age as much as they are in the States. A 22-year-old could finally get to high school after several years working in the mines, or a 45-year-old could be in a second grade class, finally learning how to read and write. Some of these students we saw looked like grown men.

I was reaching into the van when a group of high-schoolers surged around us unexpectedly, startled me and almost knocked me over. Hastily I stepped behind the driver, who was returning our equipment to the van, and the four of us were able to make our getaway. The excitement and fierce energy of those students was somewhat frightening and quite different than the docile-acting blacks back in Johannesburg. Once again I wondered if I was in the right place at the wrong time in South Africa

"Is this normal?" I asked one of the white film crew.

"This is Soweto," he replied, assuming that was sufficient

explanation.

Not long afterward, the government ruled that the language of instruction in the black schools must be Afrikaans, not English. That was the final straw. After years of government oppression, exile to the barren homelands and the loss of their rights, the new language edict triggered an explosive uprising of black students in Soweto on June 16, 1976. In response, the armed police shot and killed many of those rock-throwing pupils, thus dragging the country into years of bloody violence.

June 16 would always be a national day of remembrance.

SECTION II

Ndebele woman and child © Elizabeth Schneider

TEA AND SUGAR

Elizabeth was still making the bed, but I had prepared our tea and wanted to surprise her.

"Elizabeth, come in for tea. It's 11 o'clock."

"Miz Betty, I cain't come fer now. I'se got 'n extra flat today. Joyce, she sick," she explained.

"But I have to go to varsity soon. I've got a class. If we have our tea now, we can have a short visit," I said.

Elizabeth gave a long sigh and came in, saying resignedly, "*Yebo.*" ("*Yebo*" is the Zulu equivalent of "OK," "that's fine," and "I agree.")

Then she added, "Today Miz Wood she say we all gotta take anothah flat because Joyce not heah. We gotta be 'pahrt Joyce'."

"Sit down here, Elizabeth," I urged her, pulling out her chair. "I've got something special for our tea break."

Elizabeth sat down, eyeing the color of the tea in the cup. "You mean Rooibaas?" pronouncing it "roy-baas" "That red tea them Aferkaners drink?"

"No, I don't really like the flavor of Rooibos tea. It tastes so metallic. It's too strong a taste for me, rather bitter. By the way, do you know what Rooibos tea is made of?"

"Well," said Elizabeth, "they got them leaves in boxes, kinda like our real tea, but littler leaves, with sticks 'n stuff in it. They put it inna pan with watah 'n boil it fer a long time."

"Boil it? But I thought tea should never be boiled. Are you sure?"

Elizabeth just looked at me and said patiently, "Miz Betty, I'se wuhked for Aferkaners lots. I'se made their Rooibaas. I *know.*"

"But 'Rooibos' isn't a Zulu word; it's an Afrikaans word," I said. "Do you know what it means?"

"Red-bush. Lotsa peepul they like it. I don', but I'll drink it with lotsa 'n lotsa sugah."

"I guess the tea plant must have red leaves. Come to think of it, even their dried leaves look reddish-brown."

I walked over to the cupboard and picked up the Rooibos tea box that I had purchased for Afrikaner guests who asked for it, because it's quite a popular drink with them. I carried it over to the table where we were sitting.

"When it's made, it's a coppery-red and looks pretty in a white cup. But the smell and taste I just don't care for," I said.

"So whut you got special today fer tea?"

"We've got brown sugar to give our tea-with-milk more flavor than just ordinary white sugar. And it's healthier," I said, triumphantly.

Elizabeth, indignantly, "That stuff? Whuffo you use gov-n-munt issue' That stuff don' have no *sweet* in it!"

Startled by the vehemence of her reply, I responded, "But in America I use it all the time on my oatmeal to give it extra flavor. I thought it would be a nice change today from our usual white sugar and milk with our regular Five Roses black tea. I'm sure it's healthier, too."

Elizabeth eyed the bowl with brown sugar that I had offered her. "Guvment-issue is whut the guvment make us eat when they don' want us to use the good stuff," she said. She then added firmly and disparagingly, "But brown, not sweet. Kin I have the really-real sugah? The white stuff?"

I resignedly brought over the bowl of white sugar and put it on the table between us, handed her the sugar spoon, adding, "Here's to a good day today!"

RESEARCH ASSISTANT HILDA

"I e-x-p-e-c-t you will be all right," said tidy Prof. Hammond-Tooke, slowly leaning back in his leather chair and puffing on his pipe as I named the villages I planned to visit during my first field trip in 1976. "But bear in mind the government permit allowing you to be in the black homelands must be with you at all times, or you're illegal."

His offhand attitude belied his basic belief that the woman planning to write her thesis on "why elaborately decorate mud huts?" was ill equipped to pursue her eccentric goal. She was an American and an artist, wasn't she?

"The unrest in South Africa is volatile now and dangerous. But you will have Hilda, and she knows the territory and the languages," he said, trying to be optimistic in that jocular way Brits have. Just then Hilda Malantoa, dressed elegantly but not suitably for fieldwork, strolled in, two hours late for our departure. About 5'5" tall, solidly built, middle aged, with very dark skin, Hilda was fluent in several Bantu languages (Zulu, isiZulu, Sotho, seSotho etc.), Afrikaans and English, and was very proud (as she deserved to be) of her undergraduate degree in social science.

As the Anthropology Department's research assistant, Hilda accompanied graduate students and faculty to translate when they traveled into the bush. I was the first to ask her to drive hundreds of kilometers, then trudge in the mud where roads ended, hauling cameras, tape recorders, small gifts (dried fruit, canned tuna, etc.) to fill out questionnaires for weeks at a time.

"Why do we have to make so many trips?" she had complained when I initially told her we would need to collect 200 interviews from the rural women who decorated their mud huts so strikingly.

"My statistics advisor insists on a very rigorous approach to stratified sampling. And I always need to photograph how the respondent has painted her house."

"But even the department chair doesn't go to people's homes. We do his interviews at the nearest mission. That's so much more efficient."

"Yes, but I'm married to my statistics advisor, not Professor Hammond-Tooke."

"Hmmph," Hilda managed to reply. I could tell she was thinking something like "at least she listens to her husband." I could see she was ambivalent about her work, but continued because the pay was good and enabled her to work on her M.A. by correspondence. Most whites were naïve about life in African rural areas, so she probably assumed being a research assistant would be a breeze and could set them straight with little effort on her part. It was the beginning of a long and difficult relationship.

With Professor Hammond-Tooke's lukewarm sendoff, I loaded my box of maps, gifts, cameras, tape recorder and notebook with government permit into the boot, as South Africans called the trunk. Hilda sat nearby, bored.

"Hilda, shouldn't we check what's going on in the homelands before we start? Let's get *The Sowetan* and check the radio news before we leave," I suggested, hoping to forestall the complaints I expected about why she shouldn't have to go on this trip with me.

"I've already checked, and there've been some fires set at one of the mission schools where we're scheduled to sleep tonight," she announced glumly.

"So should we organize our trip to another area?" I hoped my can-do attitude masked my feelings of inadequacy and frustration in this situation.

"No," she sighed, "maybe things will quiet down before we get there. That village is about 200 kilometers away." With that, she climbed into the passenger's seat of my American car, whose steering wheel was on the left.

"It's on the wrong side," she informed me.

I said nothing as we set off for our two-week field trip with my reluctant companion. After a couple of hours, I asked, "How much farther to the first mission?" I was thinking how we had so much work to do. This was our first survey trip to find where the Ndebele people lived scattered across several huge magisterial districts.

Hilda replied slowly, with measured patience, "You don't have to worry. I know how to find all the missions. Don't forget, I went to a mission school in the homelands."

"I know. What was the name of your mission school?" trying to be cordial.

"Glen Elen. It's only a four-hour drive. We can stay at the priest's place tonight. Maybe even stop at a smaller mission on the way in case there's unrest going on at Glen Elen. Did you hear the news this morning?"

"I did, and I'm worried." After hours of driving on these dusty roads, I didn't relish staying in a mission that was at risk for violence. I didn't know where we'd sleep then. The car would be at risk; we'd both be at risk.

"Well, if we get close to Glen Elen, and the radio says all's not well, we can stay at my mother's place. It's not far from the mission."

"But Hilda, my government permit says 'You are not to stay with a Bantu.' I'd hate to lose my permit. It's the only way I can do fieldwork."

Hilda nodded towards the radio. "Oh, oh. Hear that? The mission was set on fire this morning and the government says 'mission closed.' Let's go to my mother's village tonight. My family's homestead has two rooms, kitchen and bedroom. And it's round with that thatched roof that you like."

"But the car? Where can we hide our bright yellow car? Won't your family be upset at you arriving unannounced with a white guest?"

"No, African families are used to unannounced visitors. After all, there's no phone out there. And being guests, we'll probably get the one bed. There's always mealie-meal for everyone."

The village was small, and the red soil surrounding it dominated the landscape. As we arrived, I tried to make the yellow car less conspicuous by parking behind some scrub bushes in the sparse sandy soil. The one communal water faucet was nearby, so we washed as much dust off as we could. I ignored the sand in my teeth, and we went in for supper.

As we ate, sitting on the floor leaning against the wall, Hilda's family and children sat there, too, eating with their fingers, African style. The corn meal porridge, called mealie-meal, was white and the dried spinach dark green. It was much tastier than I had expected, and while my finger-eating was clumsy, I was hungry and ate it all.

After supper and dead tired after the days' adventures, we adjourned to the one bed in the mud hut, just as Hilda had predicted.

I crawled in, sleepily watching Hilda adjust her panty hose over her elaborately braided cornrows. I couldn't help asking, "Why do you wear your panty hose on your head?"

"To protect the braids. This hairdo cost me a lot in Soweto, and I want to keep it smooth as long as I can," she explained as she finished tying the panty legs into a soft knot on her forehead. Hilda crawled in beside me, and as I drifted off to sleep, the dire warnings listed in the government homeland permit came to mind.

"You will not stay with a Bantu" was one of the first, and here, my first night in the field, I was not only staying with a Bantu but sleeping with one as well, thereby breaking the second stern command on the list.

ELIZABETH AND JOYCE SINGING

When Elizabeth had finished mopping the floor, we both stopped work for our morning tea. As we settled down, waiting for the teakettle to whistle, she looked over at the small radio and asked, "Don't you open the radio? She has good Zulu music that make you wanna dance."

"Put on the Zulu station then," I said reluctantly, not sure of the frequency. "Maybe there'll be news and you can explain it to me."

"*Yebo.* Heah she is. It make me dance, like I do in chuch on Satiddy night."

Just then someone knocked at the door, and Elizabeth hastily put the second teacup out of sight in case it was Mrs. Wood, the manager. Mrs. Wood was stern about the flat cleaners not eating in anyone's flat, even if the owner were there. "They must do their work, then leave for the next flat," she liked to repeat crisply.

But it was Joyce, Elizabeth's best friend who also worked in our block of flats. She came in and took the hidden teacup while Elizabeth got another. As we sat comfortably at the breakfast bar, dipping our anise seed rusks and savoring Five Roses Tea with milk and white sugar, Elizabeth continued telling about her church, while stirring her tea noisily.

"It nice, the Tapia Chuch of Lesotho."

"Why do you go to church on Saturday night?" I asked.

"The people they wuhk in day, even Sunday, so we go to chuch at night, when *ever-one* can come. We go *all* night. And we sing a lot in seSotho. I like seSotho. I can speak some. They can heah [understand] me. But the Venda speakers like Petah say, it's too heavy. It's too deep. When they say just a wuhd…like my sistah who live over that side…she and my othah sistah…they talk it – is like to read a book. We no understand. If it is just to say a leetle bit, I can 'heah' it, but if it's more — it's too much.

"In my chuch we sing in Sotho. Like seTswana [a Sotho dialect used in Botswana] it not so different, but all Sotho it is diffrent. Mosh-wesh-we people [from Lesotho], they talk diffrent. It more like seTswana, not so much like the Pedi [another Sotho dialect]. It is hard. The people from Basutoland [the nearby country now called Lesotho] talk a leetle bit different.

"Joyce, my frien' heah, we go to chuch togetha an' sing all night... We sing for *you*."

And they did. Lustily!

"Then th' music it play and we dance like this," she said as she grabbed Joyce's hand. They energetically swung around the living room, laughing, stamping and singing during their half-hour lunch break. As the rhythmic, thumping township music filled the air, I found myself pounding the table to its infectious beat.

I hoped Mrs. Wood was out shopping.

BOYFRIENDS AND TROUBLES

Elizabeth came in today, subdued, but feeling the need to talk. As she filled the electric teakettle, she turned to me and said, "Y'know my boyfriend?"

"Yes," I said. I had met him one day with Elizabeth. I was amused we shared yet another thing in common - her boyfriend was called Jack, the same as my husband.

"His brother, he dead. Satiddy night. I think it warn't so late, seven o'clock. They killed him with a *screwdriver.* Here," indicating the right side of her chest. "He was goin' t' the store for some cigarettes, I think. The boys, they saw him, and when he come outside, they stab him. For the money, I think. They saw she had money, so they take it." Elizabeth frequently confused "he" and "she" in English.

"They left him there in the street until Sunday morning; then they take him away to the mor-tiary."

"Why so long before they picked him up?" I asked, at a loss to think of what else to say in response to this gory revelation.

"They busy. They got lotsa pickin' up to do all through Soweto. They don' get there 'til morning on Sunday. I think she's goin' to be married soon, next month I think. It a shame!"

Using the water that was now boiling, she made our tea. We settled down for our daily ritual of 11 a.m. tea together. She sighed, stretched her stiff, swollen legs, and we sat down at the comfortable snack bar. She reached for the sugar and put in four spoonfuls, stirring briskly, then added quite a bit of milk.

"Y'know my mothah's lastborn? He 16 years old. He naughty. He like to drink too much. She now in jail. I called the police myself. She saw the little girl who lives with an old man. The old man is not so old, but he seek. He a patient. He walk like this," she said, demonstrating a crouched, slow shuffle. "I dunno what's wrong with him."

"My brother, he so cheeky. He come into my mothah's house, and he get a knife, a table knife I think, an' he went back to th' house where the li'l girl and th' ol' man are. Th' ol' man say, 'No, you can't take her.' So he stabbed them both, the little girl and the old man.

"My brother's so bad. I call the police myself. They take him. They don' have papers, no charges on him. But they take him away to jail for five years. This is my mothah's last born, so naughty!"

We refilled our teacups and had another anise seed rusk. This time she added five spoonfuls of sugar to her cup.

Elizabeth continued her conversation. "My boyfrien' he has a wife in Zululand. He [the wife] comes to see him in December, and now they go back to Zululand fer a visit."

She stirred her milk tea thoughtfully. "They all have wives. I don' take a man into my house unless he pay rent or help pay rent. My boyfrien', she buys me a bag of mealie-meal or sometimes a sack of coal or th' candles, but he no live with me.

"Petah, you know?" (Peter was our Venda furnace boy who also cleaned our car.) "He have two wives back theah in Louis Trichart. None heah."

Elizabeth continued, "My boyfrien' he's married. When they's married, they's no money to help you. Sometimes they give you one rand for the week -- *sometime*s. For many weeks they give you nothin'. They send it all home to th' wives." She shook her head.

"Josiah?" (He was a Zulu and the main caretaker in our flat complex.) "He has three wives. Two live here, an' one, I think lives there in Zululand. He never has no money.

"Topsy," she continued, "d'you know 'bout her?"

"That friend of yours that cleans the floors upstairs?" I said.

"Yup. She had her friend livin' with her, but he no pays

the rent. She no pays *nothing,* so Topsy say to her friend, 'You leave.' She swept him out the door," and Elizabeth vigorously demonstrated the process.

Elizabeth added four more spoonfuls of sugar to her tea, stirring noisily, then added more milk as well.

"A sack of coal c'n last five days. It is too much. A sack of coal, this much." She lifted her hand to indicate a 2' long bag of coal.

"It is so 'spensive and they want to charge moah. My train, it cost so much, five rand a month, and the food! My rent, she's R14.50, a month. R14.50 and they are closing the houses 'cause the people they don' pay the rent. They just lock 'em up and leave 'em.

Elizabeth finished her tea and said, "But you help, you and th' woman in No. 802, th' ole lady. She help me. They want to put electricity into Soweto. I don' want it. It so 'spensive. Lotsa peepul don' want it, but some peepul do."

Elizabeth gathered together our tea things, painfully stretched her swollen legs, and took our cups to the kitchen sink. I noted she was wearing old, worn bedroom slippers instead of shoes.

She said, "I'm through, missus. Thanks fer the coffee an' the blouse," one which I had given her. "I'll fix it so it fits me on the sides and here," she said, indicating her ample and gradually expanding hips.

"It's gonna be hot today."

HILLBROW EMERGENCY CLINIC

It was a Saturday night in our Braamfontein suburb of Johannesburg. Since Jack had gone back to the States for six months to finish his teaching contract at the College of San Mateo, I finally had the time to fill out endless index cards for my dissertation. I missed him but had to stay in Johannesburg because of my classes and job as Curator of the Ethnological Museum.

How quiet it is here in the flat, I thought. Our black boom box was gently playing some chamber music, which invariably set the mood for thoughtful work. True, outside on this Saturday night, the neighborhood was noisy and full of activity, but right then our little flat seemed to me an oasis of peace. I fixed a cup of Five Roses Tea, added milk (a pleasant habit I had acquired while living in this former British colony) and settled back at my desk to go to work.

After a productive half hour, there was a loud, sharp pounding on my door. Who could that be? Almost all of our friends socialized as couples, so I had become accustomed to a limited social life these six months without Jack. Puzzled, I opened the front door and saw Josiah, our night watchman, and Peter, the furnace boy. They were panting as if they had been running up the seven flights of stairs. Trying to control their breathing, they bellowed something to me, but I couldn't understand their urgent message.

Josiah again shouted, "The night watchman! That one from other building. His head, it smashed!"

"Help, need help!" added Peter in his limited English.

Peter was a Venda speaker, and his English was much less than Josiah's. Venda speakers mostly lived near the Zimbabwe border, where few black people spoke English.

Obviously there was a crisis happening in or near our

building, and probably because I was more friendly with the workers in our building than the other tenants, Josiah and Peter had come to my flat for help.

"Come to lobby," Josiah urged me in panic, and Peter nodded vigorously, wordlessly emphasizing the emergency.

We headed down in the lift, and Josiah took me to the lobby of the flats across the street. There, collapsed in a chair, was the night watchman for Carlton Flats, his head all bloody, a trickle of blood pooling around the chair legs, and the remnants of a broken bottle all around on the floor. I was shocked and slightly sickened at the sight.

"Take him to hospital. You have car!" Josiah insisted.

"I'm not going to Soweto at night," I said shakily, but firmly, knowing that Baragwaneth Hospital was deep into Soweto.

"But he *die*!" screamed Josiah. "Take him to Clinic!"

There was a low moan from the injured watchman, which added to my dilemma.

"No, I can't," I replied, not knowing exactly where he meant by using the word "clinic." I felt torn between concern for the wounded man and reluctance to get involved in this bloody mess.

"Clinic not far, not Bara in Soweto, clinic in *Hillbrow*!" Josiah insisted.

I hesitated. Hillbrow was only about 20 minutes from where we lived, but I had no idea there was a black clinic there or where it was located.

"I tell you," Josiah continued. "Jus' go up main street t' Hillbrow and it near top of street. Big, white building, big painted red cross on it."

"All right, but can you come with me?" I asked Josiah. This was an adventure I didn't look forward to experiencing alone, or rather with a bleeding, glass-embedded black stranger, especially on a Saturday night.

"Gotta wurk!" replied Josiah. "You take him or he die!"

I realized the truth of what he was telling me, so I reluctantly agreed.

"I'll have to get some towels. I'll drive my car over here, and you'll have to put him in the back seat for me."

Josiah nodded. With legs shaking, I rushed back to our building to get some towels and my keys and to lock up before I took the lift down to the basement to drive across the street to Carlton Flats to pick the patient up.

Then, I anxiously drove up the main road to Hillbrow, looking for the black emergency clinic while trying to ignore the groans of my bloody passenger. *Yes, there it was, about halfway up the hill.* It was easy to find, a well-lit square, white building with a prominent red cross painted on it. Strange, I'd never noticed it before, but then I'd never had the need to find the black clinic before.

I pulled up to the entrance and parked at the side of the entryway. *Hm-m, not too many cars here. Not many people inside? Or perhaps they walked here or took black taxis?* I thought.

The battered watchman, Guduza, was still conscious, so I helped him get out of the car, refolding the towel around his neck to keep the blood from running down his shirt. He was trembling, but I was relieved to see that he could walk, though shakily. We entered a large square waiting room filled with many black people sitting on chairs or lying on gurneys.

A black nurse came over to us and asked the watchman in Zulu what had happened. He pantomimed a blow to his head. He really was in no condition to explain what had happened and probably spoke only Venda just like Peter, so I added what information I could. She indicated two empty chairs for us in the big waiting room.

During our long wait, I had a lot of time to think and look around. I was relieved to see there seemed to be three doctors, maybe five nurses and several male attendants, all black. This was useful information in case any of the staff in our block of flats ever needed urgent medical help.

I wondered if these black doctors had been trained at our university's medical school, since Wits always made a strong effort to enroll the maximum number of black students in both the medical and dental schools that the South African government allowed.

I worried that he could die here in the waiting room. *Life is so cheap here for blacks, and for whites, too,* I thought.

The night wore on. Some of the people waiting were bleeding through their improvised bandages. Others seemed to doze off or pass out. I felt very white.

Finally, they wheeled the watchman into an examination room and asked me to wait for him. I settled back in my chair, relieved that at last he was getting medical attention, and at a black clinic a lot closer and safer than Soweto. I began to hope that this responsibility I reluctantly took on might have a positive outcome.

Suddenly, one of the male patients on a gurney deliberately rolled off his cart and, with great effort, stumbled to his feet and headed toward another male patient on a nearby gurney. A nurse, seeing the unexpected movement, rushed over and grabbed his raised arm. She did it just in time to keep him from stabbing the patient on the gurney with something in his fist. She shouted to one of the nearby male attendants, who ran over to help her force the man's arm down.

Alarmed, everyone in the room jumped up if they could. The male attendant yelled something, and people gradually sat down. When calm was restored, I asked the nurse walking past me, "What was he doing?"

She said, in English, "Those two had been fighting before they came in here, and we had just stitched both of them up and left them, but that one," pointing to the culprit, "had hidden a sharpened bicycle spoke in his pocket, and now he tried to finish the attack."

She added, "It's almost impossible for us to find that little hole when they use those spokes, and we sometimes lose the patient." With that she hurried back to the examination room.

At last my watchman patient, newly bandaged, was wheeled back into the waiting room. I got one of the male attendants to help get him into my car.

I carefully drove back to Carlton Flats to return the watchman to his building, where Josiah was still waiting for him. Peter had already returned to our flats. I drove my car back to Bridgeport, wearily realizing I would have to get the car professional cleaned the next day to remove all the blood stains. As I returned to my flat, I hoped that a cup of hot chocolate and the 24-hour chamber music station on the radio would be able to lull me to sleep.

What a night!

ELIZABETH AS INTERPRETER IN HILLBROW

It was the day that I was due to go to Hillbrow, a cosmopolitan section of Johannesburg, to meet that special Ndebele woman. She was one of my respondents who, noting my genuine appreciation of her gala beaded blanket, had offered to meet me there and perhaps negotiate a sale. I was thrilled. We made a date for our meeting the following month when my fieldwork would be over. While doing fieldwork, buying a beaded apron or blanket had seemed unethical. Many times along the way in my interviews I found myself wanting to own a few of the unique beaded fineries that made up the Ndebele woman's spectacular gala dress. Their blankets and beaded goatskin aprons were particularly beautiful, and I had certainly admired hers.

The basic unadorned woven blanket the Ndebele women purchased at the trading store was woven with four broad stripes of primary colors: blue, yellow, red and green. The women then stitched broad bands of bead designs onto the edges of these colorful wool blankets for additional decoration. The total effect was quite striking. They wore the heavy blankets, approximately 6' x 6' in size, pinned over their shoulders, letting them hang almost to the ground. Worn only by the women, they represented much expense and many months of work.

Skin aprons had two different designs. One design was for married women, the other for a new bride. For the married woman, the basic pattern consisted of a regular skin apron with two square flaps at the bottom enclosing a leather fringe between. The rest of her apron was then colorfully beaded with various designs in circles, squares, stripes and sometimes words. One phrase on an apron that had caught my eye said "Vlakfontein Pomet" spelled out in beads. It announced to her friends that she possessed a valued Identification Permit to live on Mr. Vlakfontein's farm.

Bridal aprons were more elaborate. That design had five curved flaps on the bottom that were 8 to 10 inches wide and hung in various lengths. The entire apron was often completely covered in white beads (if the woman was wealthy and could afford it). These were sewn on in 1-inch rows spread over the main part of her apron. The flaps curved at the bottom had rows of white beads sewn on in another direction. Sometimes she created a few elegant geometric designs in color, tastefully spaced among the white beads.

However, when the day came to meet in Hillbrow, I realized there would be a big problem. I didn't have the anthropology department's interpreter, Hilda, at my disposal. Hilda spoke the four languages I usually needed, Zulu, Sotho, Afrikaans and English, but that was for my official fieldwork. What to do in this situation?

Hm-m-m, Elizabeth? Might work, I thought. She didn't speak siNdebele, but siSwati, a closely related Zulu dialect. Perhaps she could do it. At least, there was a good chance I could get Elizabeth to help, and it would be an adventure for her. She loved adventures.

It seemed worth trying. So when I was having morning tea with Elizabeth, I decided to ask her. First I offered her some anise seed rusks, which she loved, then asked, "Would you like to go to Hillbrow with me today and interpret what my Ndebele friend is saying? It will help me understand her because I want to buy her blanket. I've arranged to meet her in Hillbrow a little after the noon hour. I can pay you for interpreting, just as the university pays my regular interpreter," I offered.

"Sure! Yessum, Miz Betty. Tha's gonna be fun. I can talk Zulu. Le's go," said Elizabeth, always ready for more variety in her day.

I wasn't sure this would work. There were a lot of possible problems, but it seemed to be the only way I could manage such a delicate operation.

"All right then. Meet me in the basement garage at 11:30, and I'll smuggle you into my car so we can get out of the building without Mrs. Wood seeing us," I suggested, "I'm to meet the woman at noon in Hillbrow."

Elizabeth hurried off to clean her next flat before our adventure.

Promptly at 11:30 I went down to the garage where Elizabeth was waiting behind my car. I opened the back door of the small BMW 2002, and she climbed in. As I urged her to crouch down further on the floor, I worried her girth would make it hard to keep her out of sight, but it was the best we could do.

I drove up the garage ramp with no one seeing us. A few blocks later, I parked to let Elizabeth get into the front seat with me. We headed up to Hillbrow, and I parked the car a few blocks from the Woolworth store that was our agreed meeting place. Elizabeth and I walked to the corner where my Ndebele friend was sitting on the pavement, leaning against the building with her brass-ringed adorned legs stretched out in front of her. Alongside was the ever-present plaid plastic bundle in which Ndebele women always seemed to carry their beaded treasures.

"*Saowbona, sisi,*" I greeted her, using the few Zulu words I knew, which mean literally, "I see you, sister." She responded with "*Ninjani, nina ninjani,*" which means "I see you, too."

Elizabeth greeted her as well. We then sat down on the sidewalk to negotiate. As the Ndebele woman slowly undid her bundle and the strikingly beaded blanket came to light, I was thrilled to see that it was as beautiful as I had remembered.

The negotiations started. While Elizabeth clearly was no academically trained interpreter, she somehow managed to negotiate adequately with much gesturing of "no" and some singsong-murmured "*yebo*'s."

After nearly 30 minutes, they finished talking and Elizabeth, always thrifty, worriedly told me the price the Ndebele woman was asking. It was expensive, but I really did not want to argue about it. The woman obviously needed the money, and from my trading store visits in the Homeland, I knew the price of the beads. White beads were cheaper and the colored ones more expensive, the cost depending on the color. She had used lots of the priciest colors: orange, red and blue beads. The traders knew the colors that the Ndebele women liked and hiked their prices accordingly.

But I was pleased I could afford it and happily paid her the price, about 100 rand (about $100 at the time), which was not much more than her cost of the beads.

Elizabeth, always practical, suddenly noticed a small blue bead amongst all the black beads in one part of the design. She pointed to it and presumably asked the woman in Zulu,

"Why that bead blue? That bring bad luck to my missus?" she asked sternly, referring to a popular rumor that had been going around. If an Ndebele woman was going to sell her blanket to a white woman, she would have to put a mistake into the work to forestall the bad luck that otherwise would happen to her, the seller of the blanket.

"That?" the woman said. "I ran out of black beads," Elizabeth told me later.

Sale accomplished satisfactorily, the women carefully folded the blanket into a manageable bundle that Elizabeth carefully placed on top of her head.

We bid our Ndebele friend goodbye. Elizabeth, erect, tall and dignified with the heavy beaded blanket perfectly balanced on her head, walked ahead of me on the sidewalk toward my car.

As I walked behind her and looked at her from the back seeing her erect, majestic body walking in front of me with the colorful beaded blanket balanced on her head, my heart warmed. She looked like a magnificent ship, say, the Queen Mary, sailing along the tourist route to Europe. People stopped and stared. I felt like I was returning home with the treasure of a lifetime.

FIELDWORK WITH HILDA

During my three years of intermittent fieldwork, we always stayed at a mission. Missions were the only places that Hilda and I could share a room, given that one of us was black and the other white. But even some of the missions were segregated into black and white sections. One time we were shocked to find that the white section had been set alight and burned out the day before, but the black section remained intact. We had to find another mission where we could both safely stay. Even though that morning we had checked the radio news reports as well as the black newspaper *The Sowetan,* and the news appeared fairly calm, we were uneasy. But with the violence permeating the Homelands by then, I scarcely slept, fearing this alternate mission would also be attacked. Fortunately it wasn't, but this experience did nothing to improve Hilda's distaste for fieldwork or my mixed feelings.

One day we were getting close to the small village that had caught my attention because of its historic background. The Paramount Chief of the Ndebele had fled here as a child with his mother in 1883 to hide from the Afrikaaner troops that were fighting to take over their land. I hoped to interview elderly women who might remember tales of those dark war years and could fill gaps in the history I was planning to write for my thesis. I turned to Hilda and said, "These next four interviews should add some important facts to their background. Be sure to get as much information as you can regarding their history when you're doing the interviews."

Hilda said nothing. She seemed forbidding and stern. In the distance I watched a woman getting water from the pump; put the heavy, dripping bucket on her head; hold it upright with one hand and start walking. I parked on the settlement's outskirts, planning to walk in with Hilda to do our work.

"We'll need the questionnaires and the two cameras." I said, picking up my notebook, tape recorder, cameras and gifts. I turned to see if Hilda was ready and was startled to see she was still sitting firmly in her place, not reaching for the questionnaires.

"I'm not going in," she said with determination, arms folded and mouth grim.

"What? What do you mean you're not going in?" I said, not sure I had heard her correctly.

"That's right! I'm tired of interviewing, and I'm not going out there."

"But Hilda, that's what we have to do, get interviews. We're almost finished doing them, and after four more field trips we'll be done. We won't have to drive out here any more. I can work on my thesis at home."

She said nothing. I could see she was resolute, knowing full well her value to me and had decided to revolt. It was frustrating, and I did not know what to do. I sat there wondering what other field workers did in a case like this. She knew her power. This was her territory, the people spoke her language, and if I didn't have her help, I wouldn't be able to finish my fieldwork.

As we sat in stony silence, I turned over several plans of action in my mind, but none seemed to fit. Driving back to the mission wouldn't help. Who knew enough English to help me? Leave Hilda out there? But then I suddenly realized *I had the car*. It was an hour's drive back to the mission, and Hilda wouldn't walk that far. I played my next card.

"OK, you refuse to go into the village. Then we will just sit here until you decide to do the work you are being paid to do." With that I leaned back, firm in my resolve, and sat there, single-minded and furious.

We sat thus for 45 long minutes, the longest minutes I've ever spent. We said nothing and didn't look at each other. Finally, with a long sigh, Hilda said, "Let's go." She got out of the car and picked up the questionnaires. I picked up the cameras, tape recorder, gifts and my notebook and we started our short hike into the village. I approached the old woman at the first homestead, greeting her first as is the custom.

Surprisingly, Hilda did her work in her usual professional manner, settling down on the mud bench and beginning her conversation with the respondent by explaining who we were and what we wanted. We finished our four interviews as planned.

Hilda and I never mentioned the incident again. She continued to work with me until the fieldwork was completed, but our relationship was based on a new foundation. I had increased empathy after her attempted revolt and always gave her a gift at the end of each field trip with my sincere thanks. On her part, she continued to interview, yet that boundary of lowly graduate student versus paid research assistant was now more palpable and honored. We worked together until the end, but our relationship remained difficult.

MUTI SHOPPING

"Elizabeth, I have some errands to do in the center of Joburg. Would you like to go downtown with me?" I asked.

Elizabeth often had things she needed in town, but with the long hours of her flat-cleaning job in our building, she seldom had spare time to do anything in town other than rush for her train home or bustle off to work.

"Miz Betty, you know I wanna go, but Miz Wood is all upset today. She'll holler if she can't find me."

This was true. Mrs. Wood, in her conscientious, busybody way, took her building-manager job seriously in Bridgeport, our block of flats. If I wanted to give Elizabeth some time in downtown Johannesburg, we were going to have to organize it better. This would take time and the cooperation of the other "'gulls," as Elizabeth called her fellow workers.

"OK, Miz Betty. I need to get some muti for my muthah, and the doctah downtown has good muti for her. Le's go."

I hadn't been to a traditional Zulu medicine store before, so this sounded interesting. The first part of our plan worked fine. Elizabeth alerted Joyce and another of her friends to divert Mrs. Wood for the fairly short time she would be gone. I went down to my little yellow BMW 2002, warmed up the motor and had the back door open for when Elizabeth would appear. Fortunately, Josiah, the building watchman, was nowhere to be seen. Both Elizabeth and I felt sure that he was an informer who would cheerfully give her away to Mrs. Wood if pressed.

A few minutes later a rather breathless Elizabeth appeared, having covered the green uniform with her ragged coat. As I helped her kneel down on the floor, all 200-plus pounds of her, I hoped our luck would hold and Josiah would not see us as I drove up out of the garage into the alley. It wasn't easy making Elizabeth invisible from outside the small car. It was not that roomy in the back, and the windows might reveal that someone was trying to hide on the floor. But we didn't have much time to worry about that. It was more important to get out of the garage before Josiah showed up. I drove up the ramp and out the garage door.

After a few streets I pulled over to the side of the road and released Elizabeth from her cramped position so she could get into the front seat with me.

"Whew! Tha's scary. Miz Wood fire me fer sure if she see me," said Elizabeth.

We proceeded downtown. After parking my car and picking up the package that had been sent to me at the American Consul General's office, I said to Elizabeth, "Now where do we go for your muti?"

Following her directions to the traditional medicine store, we walked several streets to the black section of town, not far from the train station. I was totally unfamiliar with that area. This was the Johannesburg known to all the blacks and where they shopped. They passed through it each day as they came in from Soweto on their way to work.

As we passed some fresh produce, I noticed that the price was much more reasonable than any I had ever seen. Elizabeth paused to buy some. I was attracted by the prices, so I wandered over to a spot where I had seen some ripe avocados. There was a sign in Zulu above the avocados that I couldn't understand. When I asked Elizabeth what it said she laughed and tried to translate for me, but that was even more incomprehensible. Finally, around on the other side of the artistically stacked avocados, I saw it in English.

"Don't play piano on the avos," it warned sternly.

After a few blocks we arrived at an old building with a small doorway that had no sign that I could see.

"There he is," she said, opening the door. "That's wheah the doctuh has his muti. We go in."

The room was fairly large. Although it was dimly lit, I could see shelves that held rows of vials holding different colored powders, and bins that were filled with a strange assortment of roots, leaves, animal teeth and several kinds of animal paws. To one side I could see a snakeskin hanging on the wall. The Zulu labels were incomprehensible to me.

As Elizabeth was talking to the traditional doctor, I couldn't help but admire the lulling, seductive sound of their Zulu words, wistful that I couldn't understand. The occasional clicks in the language intrigued me, and I vowed to work harder in my Zulu class so I could master what I had learned were the four different clicks they were using. So far I had mastered one click, but the subtleties of the other three were elusive.

Elizabeth made her purchase, and the traditional doctor, who wore a colorful Swazi cloth tied over one shoulder to indicate his profession, wrapped her muti carefully in newspaper. We hurried back to my car. It was getting late. We had had good luck so far on our downtown adventure, but we couldn't count on it lasting much longer. It was high time to get back to our building before Mrs. Wood noticed Elizabeth was gone.

ALYSSA'S PROJECT

Alyssa, my fellow graduate student at the university, turned with a relieved sigh from her fortress of books in the research library. "There's the bell. Let's take our tea outside under the jacaranda tree," she suggested. "I've got a project I need your ideas and help with."

We adjourned to the outer lawn, carrying our Five Roses milk tea with us. As we settled down on the grass, she sketched out her plan. "When I get back to Israel, I'm writing a children's book about a young African boy and his life here, but I need to have pictures – that's your role – and need to find the boy and perhaps his mother for the models. Do you have any ideas about how to get them? What about your maid, Elizabeth, and that big family of hers you're always talking about?"

"Sounds possible," I said, immediately recognizing this project as one where Elizabeth could not only recruit the necessary models, but would warm to such an idea even without pay, although Alyssa had said she would pay them. "Let me talk to her tomorrow, and I'll let you know."

Next day, while Elizabeth ironed Jack's tennis shorts with a much-too-hot iron that gave them a slightly ochre overtone, I broached the question. "Elizabeth, I have a good friend that is writing a book about Africa, and she needs to have some pictures. Do you think you could bring a young boy here this weekend so I can take some pictures of him doing some things?" I was not sure how much I should tell her about it.

"Ow-w-ee," she responded, "I think I ask Figula. She have a fine Umfana. He five. I ask."

"What's his name?" I asked.

Elizabeth looked at me pityingly for my lack of Zulu vocabulary. "*Umfana* – 'boy'" she repeated. "Name 'Umfana' mean 'boy'."

"You mean he's just called 'boy'?"

"*Yebo.* Figula have three children, but first two gulls, and when boy come, they call him 'boy', that's Umfana. They so happy. I ask Figula just now."

The next day Elizabeth didn't yet have the answer. I settled back, realizing an African's time frame differs from Alissa's and mine. Her "I ask Figula 'just now'" meant sometime soon, either a day or a few days later. But if she had said, "I ask Figula 'now, now'," it would have meant much sooner, either right away when she got home or certainly that evening or next morning. I repeated the conversation verbatim to Alyssa, but she didn't recognize the crucial difference in meaning.

"Oh dear! If you can't get Elizabeth, what am I going to do about this weekend?" she fretted.

"I assure you, Alyssa, that things are moving ahead. We certainly will get our models from Elizabeth, but we must wait a bit."

By the following day Elizabeth had talked to Figula, who agreed to let Umfana come. Elizabeth kept chuckling at the idea of a day in the park with "pichers 'n everthin'.' Alyssa, when she heard, heaved a sigh of relief, so we set about planning what things we should photograph that would visually carry out the story she planned.

"Pink cotton candy, for sure," she said smiling, "after the merry-go-round." I thought Umfana would like that.

We contentedly sat back to work on her storyboard.

AFRICAN NAMES

I opened the bag of anise seed rusks while Elizabeth filled our teacups. We settled down for a little chat, and I watched Elizabeth put in four spoonfuls of sugar. She had something on her mind, I could see, as she reached out for a fifth spoonful. We each poured in our milk.

As we stirred companionably, she shook her head and said, "My li'l boy Albert, he sick. He ate somethin', I don' know. They took him to Bara (Baragwaneth Hospital for Africans) and operate on him. They make a big hole, from heah to heah," she said, gesturing from her left rib area to groin. "It were too much. They put a pipe in him, and he has green water. Green like that there," pointing to my chartreuse towel. "Plenty water. They take him home from Bara. Bara's too full of people. Plenty people. He mus' go home, an' when he get some bettah, he go back to doctah. But he go back to Bara today. He too sick. He eat somethin'. I don' know."

"Is he feeling better now?" I asked.

"*Yebo*," she nodded. "He say he bettah now, and he eat some. But he scream! But doctah give pills to make the hurt stop. Albert, he hurt, so he cry," she continued. She sat there worriedly and drank some tea.

"Will you call the hospital and see if he bettah?" she asked.

"Yes, I'll call. How is he registered? Albert? Or under his Swazi name?" I asked.

"He called Albert there. But he have Swazi name like I have."

"What is your Swazi name?" I asked, temporarily postponing a hospital call, which could be a complicated event.

"Ah, ow-w…it too heavy. I bring you my passbook and you see. Swazi name is too much. Too heavy," said Elizabeth.

"Who gives you English names?"

"At the clinic, they don' like our name. *They* give you a name. The sistah, they say who you are. They make three names. They give you English name first, they write down. Then they give you Swazi name and then family name...one, two, three."

"What was your first-born's name?" I ask, referring to her eldest child.

"Gertrude. Her name is *Togo*. It mean 'heppy.' I's so heppy when I born her," she said, looking out the window as memories absorbed her.

"So who gave her the name Gertrude?"

"My madam I wukked for then. She say Gertrude."

"And your second-born?" I asked, refilling my teacup.

"Lucy. Th' clinic give her name 'Lucy.' Her name is *Salukazi*. It is from granny," which she pronounced "grainee," and indicating a gray-haired grandmother by stroking her turbaned hair.

"The next child?"

"My nex' she is Agnes. You know Agnes. She come here to see you. The clinic say her name Agnes. I name her *Flazana*. It was raining so hard when I born her, so I call her *Flazana*.

"Then Ernest, the clinic nuhse give him name Ernest." A big broad smile creased her face. "I call him *Umfana*...boy." (A famous Zulu soccer player is called Umfana Umfana, literally Boy Boy.)

"The nex' is David. His fathah's boss give name. I call him *Um-zwaki*, it mean 'home.'

"Nex' is Betty. I gave her name. My mothah she call her *Usi-piwa* for gift, but it is for me I name her, and her name is *Kap-sili*. It mean *Usa-gubisa*. Why? I don' know; too heavy. Whut can I say?"

Upon checking my Zulu dictionary later, I noted that it means 'pride'.

Having heard the names of six, I assumed that was all the children Elizabeth had.

"Don' you wanna know more? I got plenty children. I got more."

"How many do you have?" She lifted her left hand, palm out, and began counting, starting at the little finger.

"I got seven children, plenty. Then I have Albert. I give it to him, his name, but he is *Un-dhlandhla*, Lucky Boy."

"And what is your mother's name?" I asked.

"Lenah. But her Swazi name is too, too heavy. It *Ma-bunduru.*"

"And your name, Elizabeth, came from where?"

"My mothah's madam, from a place called Piet Retief, give me that name. She my little mother. But my Swazi name is *Ko-koyi.* It because my mothah's sister say to my mothah, 'You like to cook with this'," she said while pointing to a large tin canister. "Call her that name, Ko-koyi. So when she born me, she call me Ko-koyi."

"Why-foah you ask all this? You like Zulu names?" asked Elizabeth, puzzled, looking at me questioningly.

I nodded and reached for the phone to call Baragwaneth Hospital to find out how Albert was today.

"He's better, Elizabeth," I reported after the call, and we both finished our tea, relieved.

NEPHEW JOSEPH IN BARAGWANETH HOSPITAL

One day Elizabeth was doing extra laundry in the tub for us. As I was preparing our tea, Jack murmured on his way out, "Better make it strong. Elizabeth has been drinking." I had noticed she had been quite talkative and having difficulty with her words.

As we settled down to tea, Elizabeth (stirring in six spoonfuls of sugar instead of four), said worriedly, "Please call th' hospital about my sistah's little boy Joseph. He eat somethin.' We take no notice, but he vomit so much he like this." She illustrated by swaying limply back and forth, her head rolling, eyes closed.

"The ambulance she come and take her to Bara [Baragwaneth Hospital] yestiddy. I think she die. She so little." Elizabeth held her hand vertically with fingers together and upward, in typical South African fashion to show age or size. (This gesture, with the palm held vertically, indicated height for people, whereas the hand held horizontally indicated height of animals or objects.)

"Please, you call with *youah* words. They no lissen to mine. I'ze so worried. My sistah, she seek [sick]. She cry so much all night. She sleep in my mothah's bed and she cry. She say her childern all get seek and they die. 'They die like glass,' she say. 'They all die (Elizabeth swept her arm over a vast area to indicate grass) like glass,'" (using "L" for "R" in English, as Zulu speakers often did.)

I started gathering information for making the call for her. "How old is Joseph?" A phone call to Baragwaneth was a big production. When someone did respond, you had to have all details available: what day he was brought in, how he appeared, and from where.

Elizabeth continued, "He seek [sick] one day from school.

I dunno what she eat. His mouth it look terrible. He always.... childern always hungry, so they eat I dunno what. At school he pick somethin' up an' eat it. His stomach, she pulls hard."

"I have the numbah here wheah she is." After patting both bosoms, she pulled out a crumpled paper with writing on it. On the paper one person had written "Joseph Sithole," her nephew's name. Another had written "hole [ward] 17, hospital." Elizabeth assured me that was where he was. "He theah. You call, see if he dead."

After much delay -- transferring of calls, babies crying, phone respondent not speaking English -- I found out "Joseph, the little boy, has pneumonia." A further suggestion was to call Suster [sister, the nurse] on Ward 17. I got through on my second attempt after the line went dead on the first.

A black nurse answered my questions by responding with "Name? From where was he brought? Jabulani?" Then, quietly, "Yes, he came in yesterday. He's very weak. He's had a drip. The treatment is not effective yet." Then, "Who's calling? Who are you??"

I tried to explain that the boy's mother is the sister to my part-time cleaning woman, but that was too complicated.

The nurse dismissed me as being the madam of the mother and proceeded with more information. In a low voice, she said, "The doctor has not come yet to see him, but the mother can come at visiting hours today at 2 p.m., also Sunday, Tuesday and Thursday. Then we can tell her."

I knew the mother could not get off work during the week, but Saturday and Sunday she would go.

This information was given and taken by both of us with subdued ah-h's, um-m-mm's and oh-h's, the reassuring, sympathetic murmurings that we used following each sentence. It was the typical musical sound to all conversations between blacks, and it was what I had learned to do. It was the lubrication that assisted all exchanges. Such tone of conversation was appropriate to this sort of information exchange -- low, concerned, sympathetic.

The nurse continued after some prodding, "The boy is still

quite weak, but I think he's not too sick."

I reassured Elizabeth, "While Joseph is sick, he can be visited today, and at the moment, he is being washed in the bathroom."

Then, to cheer her up, I affirmed, "Sister thinks he will be better, and a doctor told me that Bara is a good hospital."

"Yes, it's good" Elizabeth agreed. "They sleep on floor sometimes, but they give muti and injections to make you bettah."

I knew from taking Elizabeth shopping that muti was medicine that traditional healers (*sangomas*) gave their patients—usually dried roots, bark, animal parts, and more. Who would have thought that South African hospital staff could be so accommodating as to offer not only western medicine but also, to black patients, traditional medicine as well?

ELIZABETH'S FINANCES

As Elizabeth and I relaxed in the cozy kitchen just out of sight of the front door (in case Mrs. Wood came looking for her) we both sighed companionably as the milk tea fragrance wafted up.

Passing her the sugar bowl, I said, "I thought you might like to again try a different taste in your tea. If it isn't sweet enough, put in more spoonfuls." I hoped that this time the brown sugar I offered might be acceptable.

She promptly put in three extra spoonfuls, stirring more noisily than usual to emphasize her disapproval.

To soften the blow, I put four Lorna Doone shortbread cookies along with the rusks. They seemed to help. As we dunked our rusks, she said, "Finally Miz Wood give us a raise."

I fervently hoped it was a good one because previously her salary scarcely covered the basics she had to buy. For cleaning eight flats she got R52 monthly. The management kept 70 cents (perhaps for insurance). Her train fare was R5, rent was R14.50, a sack of coal (which lasted one to two weeks) for her cook stove was R2.50, candles R2, mealie-meal (cornmeal, "our food") was R7 for a large sack that would only last a month.

"They's no money fer shoes. The exercise books [note books], fees, school uniforms, they very 'spensive," she said. "I c'n only send three of my seven childern to school," she sighed. "If I be lazy, we don't eat," she said, ending the conversation.

Afterward I mentally tallied up the money she earned doing extras for us, washing curtains R10, spotting carpets R5, laundry and ironing R15, and decided we would have to dream up other chores for her. That was the situation a year ago.

Today, Elizabeth resignedly announced that the new monthly salary would be R68.90 (management evidently takes R1.10 this year) up from the R60 most of the past year. But Elizabeth's costs had gone up, too. Her rent was now R20, not R14.50. The train was still R5, but mealie-meal, a sack of coal and candles all cost more due to the escalating inflation. I didn't ask about the children's school uniforms and the cost of the school, because whatever the cost, her raise would never be enough.

She rose heavily out of her chair, favoring her swollen legs, to wash up the tea things. I had a class to teach at the university and had to leave.

"Thanks fer breakfast, Miz Betty. Why don' you open up th' radio befoah you go?" she asked. "I like heppy Zulu music."

NEWS ABOUT GRACE

The teakettle's shrill whistle pierced the air as Elizabeth finished mopping the floor. I stopped typing and came into the kitchen to share our fragrant tea. Elizabeth looked at me questioningly while sipping her tea.

"Do they have bootchas (butchers) in your country? Yez? Must be a big city," said Elizabeth, stirring her tea thoughtfully.

"How much cost the meat? Like heah, pricey?"

"Maybe more, even," I replied. "A whole filet costs maybe 25 rand!"

"Woo-woo," she shook her head in disbelief.

We settled back. Elizabeth put in her milk and started with five spoonfuls of sugar. Clearly she had some disturbing news to share.

"I no know what happen. Grace, my frien', she is tol' to go. End of nex' week, she mus' go." Grace was Mrs. Winter's wash girl. The Winters lived downstairs from us and ran a bakery around the corner.

Elizabeth continued. "Mrs. Wintah, he said, just like that, 'Nex' week you finish. You go.' Grace say, 'No more to say to me?' Mrs. Wintah say, 'No, nothin'. Nex' week you go.'" Elizabeth demonstrated Mrs. Winter's finger shaking in Grace's face.

"Somethin' must've happen. I dunno. I just do my floo-ah. I don't do nothin' else. Mrs. Wintah, he turned and sez to me, 'On Satiddy you no come,'" Grace had told Elizabeth.

Elizabeth continued with her own problem over the weekend. "So I can't get in to do my floo-ah. Mrs. Wintah downstairs, ready to go (to their caravan home in Bronkhorstspruit, their weekend retreat) but I can't get in. *They* have key. I no have key. She not have time to lemme in."

The flat cleaners had to turn in their keys each week day to management and weren't issued keys on weekends.

"The ba-a-a-s, Mr. Wintah, he come in sudden, quick, when I there to pay foah cuhtains." (Mrs. Winter had sold Elizabeth some drapes for R50, and Elizabeth was paying this slowly off each month.)

"He say to me, 'What *you* heah for? Why you come?' I 'splain I pay foah cuhtains. He say, 'Pay n' leave. Don' you come an' visit with Grace.' Somethin' happen at shop, I think. I saw he mad. He say to Grace, 'Open yoah purse. I wanna see whut's inside.' Grace, she come again at lunch. Miz Wintah say, 'Open yoah purse again.' Somethin' happen, I think. He's opening all the drawahs like this (demonstrating desk-drawer opening.) Someone pinch, I think. They have long fingahs," Elizabeth said, using her general description of thieves.

"Some day, Miz Wintah she tell me what happen. Yestiddy she no say goodbye to Grace. To me when I come at 7:30, she laugh and talk, but when Grace she come at 8, Miz Wintah no say nothin' more. We say goodbye to the babies and John when he go to school, but Miz Wintah no say goodbye to Grace. Only to me. I dunno what happen.

"I tol' Grace nevah to have tea or nothin' there. When she want tea, go to th' shop." She paused and then suddenly got an idea. "The television, *she* talk! Yez, they see things on television. I think the Wintahs have something theah that sees what goes on. I dunno how it wuhks, but they know what goes on. The television, it see and talk. I think there's somethin' there in the place," she paused thoughtfully as she looked into the distance. "When they go fer five days, they always know what goes on. I don' do nothin' there, just my floo-ahs. I tol' Grace not to cook or nothin."

"Why they look in her purse when she theah one year, almost two? They nevah look befoah."

After a long pause, she concluded, "If Grace she steal, she not wait fer now!" Elizabeth shook her head and then reached for the teapot.

NDEBELE VISITORS

What a curious view, I thought, looking up at my high transom windows above the kitchen stove. It was usually only a view of the sky and a sliver of something really tall that might be moving along the outside corridor leading to my door. But this looked like a bouncing parade of those ubiquitous plastic bags that black people carried on their heads. The bags, always red, white and blue plaid with zipper tops, usually held an enormous number of things that the owner needed or wanted to carry along with her.

Elizabeth, of course, often carried one, but she had already finished her chores in my flat, and I didn't expect anyone else to come by.

Then when I heard the loud knocking, I wondered whether I should answer the door. Unfortunately, we hadn't yet invested in a heavily barred outer door, as most flat dwellers had, which safely permitted the owner to respond to callers or leave the main wooden door ajar on hot days.

But curiosity always won in unusual situations. I opened the door to find three traditionally dressed Ndebele women beaming at me, balancing their stuffed plastic bags atop their heads. They were in their typical dress, consisting of a blanket with broad stripes of red, yellow, green and blue pinned over the shoulder, and were wearing their marriage neck rings of copper and brass, stacked from chin to clavicle. Showing beneath the blanket were a blouse and a beaded leather apron indicating their marital status. Ndebele women, in their handsome finery, always commanded respectful and sometimes amazed stares from onlookers.

"*Saubona!*" they greeted me, which meant "I see you" in Zulu.

"*Ninjani*" I replied, which meant "and I see you, too," and opened the door wide, inviting them in.

By my visitors' use of the familiar form of greeting, I was astounded to recognize that these were some of my respondents from my most recent field trip to the Homeland. 'Homeland' was what the South African government had named that highly restricted tribal area. But how had these Ndebele women *possibly* found me here in Johannesburg?

This day my dilemma was I didn't have Hilda, my usual interpreter, here at home. My Zulu at this point consisted only of the basic courtesy greetings one used when greeting, thanking and bidding people farewell -- socially lubricative, but not very informative.

Mindful of my manners, since Ndebele women always offered me hot tea during interviews, I knew I should do the same for them in my home. As they settled comfortably on the floor in a circle, with their legs covered in heavy metal rings out straight in front of them, I went to the kitchen to heat the teakettle and find some biscuits.

My angst increased as I realized that without Hilda I sorely needed Elizabeth to help with the translating even though her home language was siSwati, another Zulu dialect. But I didn't know where Elizabeth was this afternoon. So I went to the front door and called to Joyce, Elizabeth's best friend, who happened to be walking past.

"Please get Elizabeth quickly!" I urged Joyce. I hurried back to the kitchen to begin setting up the teacups, milk and sugar, while genuinely distraught about how I would manage this language situation if Elizabeth couldn't be found. There was no time to refer to my English/Zulu dictionary; I would have to wing it.

I returned to my seat on the floor in the center of the room among my Ndebele guests. As I walked back in, the now-surreal vista of my living room struck me. Jack and I had furnished it in the manner most useful for our university life: two large desks, two posture swivel chairs, two four-drawer file cabinets and a tall bookcase for each of us, one set on each side of the room. For our social life, I had found a small two-seater rattan couch and two armchairs that were clustered around a small, non-descript coffee table. They were placed in a conversational grouping at the end of the room, the only space left, near the windows and glass door leading to the balcony. The main feature in the room, reflecting the main part of our lives, was our desks and their attachments.

But now, there were my three colorfully attired Ndebele visitors, having settled on the floor in the middle of the room, with their metal marriage neck rings showing above their shoulder blankets. Their legs, stretched out straight in front of them, were firmly encased in solid copper and brass metal rings from ankle to knee and pointed to the center of their circle. They couldn't even cross their legs because the heavy metal rings limited flexibility. The overall contrast of the colorfully dressed women with the usual office furniture in my living room made the room seem incongruous. Swivel chairs? Paper-stacked desks? They were no match for my dignified visitors, sitting erect and calm in their finery with their colorful bundles placed beside them.

They talked among themselves, occasionally looking in my direction and smiling. They seemed to be commenting on how this white woman lived, pointing to a posture swivel chair and holding their hands over giggling mouths as they viewed its strange contortions. They were too polite to go into the kitchen where women's usual chores were done, but they craned their necks, trying to see what created the high whistle the tea kettle was now sounding.

Just then, on cue, I heard Elizabeth's key in the lock and felt an enormous surge of relief as she walked in. Elizabeth would be able to handle this.

"Ow-w-w, woo woo!" she exclaimed as she looked around the room, using her phrase for a surprising or unexpected situation.

"Elizabeth, these are some Ndebele friends from the village that I visited last week." Elizabeth smiled, clapped her hands together to greet the visitors, and then went to the kitchen to calm the teakettle and finish setting out our mid-afternoon tea and biscuits. As she brought them in she confided, "Maybe they're from Ten-Morgan village where Gertrude lives, now she's married," said Elizabeth, referring to her eldest daughter. She set down the refreshments for the guests. "I'll ask them."

Elizabeth sighed as the rapid conversation slowed after her question. "No, that's not where Gertrude live," she concluded.

The women and Elizabeth were now talking animatedly to each other. I watched in envy, wishing I could understand what was going on. As we sipped our tea, conversation among the black women continued. I asked Elizabeth to find out from them how they had found where I lived.

That triggered another animated conversation. When Elizabeth spoke, they listened, but often had to question each other to clarify what she had asked, the usual small confusion with different dialects. Again, this provoked much laughter. Elizabeth seemed puzzled as well, but tried to explain to me what they were telling her.

"She say you gave her paper with numbahs on it, and that's how she know."

I thought back on what had gone on during my last field trip. I remembered at that point I was trying to clarify Ndebele art style and needed to define simple as contrasted to complex elements in a design unit on a decorated mud hut. On that field trip, when I had finished analyzing one of the Ndebele women's homesteads, one of my respondents had asked to keep the sketch I had made explaining my design system. She had asked for my sketch, even though she couldn't read. Unknowingly, I had used one of the university's note pads that had our home address printed on it. It must have been that piece of paper, which these women had found someone to read and then explain how to find where we lived in Johannesburg, a city of more than 3 million people.

During my fieldwork I had photographed their

homesteads as well as their traditional dress worn during a gala wedding event, and they had noted my deep interest in the customary small doll given to the bride. These miniature dolls were supposed to bring good luck to the bride so that she would have many children.

Their plastic bundles contained an assortment of touristy small dolls, some beaded neckties and even a beaded watch. They had planned, as traveling Ndebele saleswomen, to bring their current assortment of tourist objects, an important source of income, when they traveled into Johannesburg.

Unfortunately, such kitsch was not what I had been admiring. In their village, when there was a serious event such as a wedding, the older women worked long and lovingly on authentic wedding dolls that were a far cry from the tourist creations that they sold when they were grouped on a busy street corner in town. They had confused my cultural interest with tourist interest, and I didn't know how to handle this situation. What complicated things was that Elizabeth didn't know the difference between tourist and authentic traditional dolls either, so I was faced with a dilemma with few alternatives.

"Looky at the sparkly dolls," Elizabeth observed admiringly as the Ndebele women unpacked their bundles. She was particularly taken with the flamboyant, glittery beads that adorned the tourist dolls, in contrast to an unobtrusive traditional doll she had seen that I had purchased earlier at Operation Hunger. Operation Hunger was an outlet in town that tried to help the rural women by selling traditional beads at a reduced rate versus the substantial markup used in a village-trading store.

To the admiring "oooo's and ahh's" of Elizabeth, my visitors positioned a good-sized assortment of dolls grouped around the remnants of our afternoon tea. It was a difficult situation for me, and Elizabeth was no help. As I hopefully waited for a real, traditional wedding doll to appear, I soon realized that this was not to be. It was amusing to see the concept of a gentleman's tie reproduced in beads, as was seeing a beaded wristwatch, complete with hour hands marked in black beads, but these were the very things I had no interest at all in purchasing.

"How real, an' purty," Elizabeth said admiringly, stroking the two prominent bosoms created from glitzy beads attached to the chest of one of the dolls.

The creator also had replicated copper neck rings and metal leg and arm rings by securely wrapping copper wire around the doll's neck, legs and arms. In comparison, a traditional modest wedding doll would have had her entire body encased in small opaque colored beads. There would have been no legs because the traditional triangular body shape would have had only beaded rings neck to floor. Nor would there have been realistic hands or arms on the traditional doll, only a long, flexible beaded strip ending in grass arm rings, all done in opaque, subdued, tasteful beads. A traditional doll might also have had two small goatskin aprons with a beaded waistband, and shaped leather flaps indicating what status the married woman was at the time -- new bride, married woman, second wife or widow.

In sharp contrast, the commercial doll had gaudy beaded balls for hands carrying a beaded basket in one hand and perhaps a vegetable in the other. Her feet were formed of two beaded balls, all extravagantly highlighted with glittery, reflective beads presenting a gaudy, showy tourist doll that really offended me. But what was I to do?

The women were patiently waiting for me to choose something and were particularly encouraged by Elizabeth's obvious admiration for their offerings.

"My, what a lot of work has gone into these," I said, lamely. I'm not sure how Elizabeth translated that, but I suspect glowingly. As I picked one of the more ornate offerings, I reluctantly asked, "How much?"

Elizabeth didn't need to translate my question. The woman quickly told Elizabeth the price she was asking as I put it down. I further realized with some dismay I would have to purchase something from each one of them. I looked over all of their offerings, my heart sinking.

I took the gaudiest of the wedding dolls, picked out a beaded tie and wristwatch, being careful to purchase something from each of them. Purchase time over, I looked over at Elizabeth as she reluctantly watched the rest of their tourist items go back into their bags. Later I shared my purchases with her, giving her the tie and wristwatch.

Elizabeth began collecting the tea things and carried them into the kitchen, and we all smiled at each other, market day now over.

As they got up to leave, it occurred to me these village women probably had come up to the seventh floor by stairs, not being familiar with lifts. Elizabeth, the city woman, explained to them we would all go down to the lobby in the staff lift, and she led the way. It seemed prudent for me to join the group, since it was quite likely the flat manager, Mrs. Wood, might appear on the scene at any moment. To save Elizabeth's job, it would be politic for me to be there along with the group.

As we walked down the corridor to the lift, fortunately Mrs. Wood was nowhere to be seen, and we all gathered in the elevator. The Ndebele women were obviously disturbed and frightened by getting into the small box that was the staff lift. When the door slammed shut, there were several squeals of terror as the lift started down. Elizabeth, bless her generous heart, explained, "It's OK. We go up and down like this," I think she said, smiling reassuringly.

The village women accepted her reassurances cautiously, but clutched each other as the lift started its downward journey. I've never felt the transportation between the floors in our flat building was unusually jerky or fast, but to the visitors, this was obviously a fiendish device to end their lives. With a concerted gasp, they rode the lift to the lobby floor. A great sigh of relief exploded from all of us as the door opened safely.

First, the Ndebele women, amazed they had survived this devil's device transporting them down stairs; me, utterly grateful Mrs. Wood hadn't appeared during this operation to further condemn the disruption the Schneiders had visited upon her building; and Elizabeth, thankful that Mrs. Wood didn't know she had skipped one of her flat cleanings to help me entertain my country visitors.

SOWETO TEA TALK

While carrying groceries home from the OK Bazaar one morning, I remembered my initial reaction to that cramped, unattractive "superstore" when we first arrived in South Africa three years earlier. The only redeeming feature was its proximity to our flat, only five blocks away. The grocery store's squalor was almost enough to consider moving to another neighborhood, but instead I usually drove to more attractive grocery stores.

Location ranked high. From our flat we could walk to the university, stop by the bank next door and use the nearby post office despite their prominent signs over one entrance "Nie Blankes" in Afrikaans, meaning no whites should enter that door. That sign, posted all over South Africa, indicated that, legally, no whites could enter that particular door, whether banks, bathrooms, auditoriums, movie houses or any gathering place. Jack and I made a point of always entering *that* door, defying the strict South African segregation laws.

It was on principle. We were firmly against apartheid, so we regularly used that door, just as we always used the "Staff Only" lift, instead of the "Residents Only" lift in our block of flats. "Staff" was the euphemism the building owners used for black workers like Elizabeth and Josiah who maintained and guarded our block of flats.

The staff lift in our block of flats was usually crowded with cleaning women laughing and talking animatedly. I found it completely frustrating that I could not understand Zulu.

"Are they talking about their madams?" I once asked Elizabeth.

"Sure!" she replied, "Why not?"

Soon I enrolled in a Zulu class, which was required for the

Ph.D. at our university, and took it for two and a half years. I learned that Zulu was the second largest language of the broad Bantu family of languages. Zulu was spoken as a first language by about one-fourth of the total population of South Africa and as a second language by another fourth. It was the only language family in the world using implosive sounds, or inhalation while speaking, whereas all other languages of the world were spoken only while exhaling. Zulu was written using the Roman alphabet. After apartheid was abolished in 1994, literacy grew considerably.

Once, as I got into the lift with two of the maids, the lift unexpectedly headed down toward the basement garage. One maid, startled, screamed something in Zulu as the lift descended abruptly and then laughed to cover her embarrassment.

From the basement, the lift then went back up, and I got off at the seventh floor. I was relieved to get home, drop my groceries and contemplate having a nice cup of tea with Elizabeth.

As Elizabeth fixed tea, she agitatedly told me about her close friend Joyce.

"Joyce's sistah, she come from Zululand with husband an' three children because she is seek-seek [very sick]. She sleep for three days an' not wake up. So husband brings her to doctah heah in Joburg." Elizabeth started her story, using only the present tense as usual.

"Her husband an' frien' sitting on bench at Jabulani creche in Soweto an' talkin'. Two young men come, sat across from them, then jus' shot them here and here, *dead,*" Elizabeth said, indicating two holes, one in her forehead and the other near her left eye.

Elizabeth continued, "A boy sittin' there, they tol' him to leave. When he come back, the husband and frien' was lying down dead with blood shinin' in a little stream running down. The sun shines on it so," she said, indicating the path of blood with her hand. Her voice trailed off as she thought about it.

"So much blood ever'where. The young shootin' men jes got up and *walked* away. No one stop 'em. They all scared to be shot. They jes walk slowly away like this," and Elizabeth, despite her weight, aptly demonstrated an arrogant, slow walk.

"We sat with Joyce's seek sistah until middle of night. She cryin' and cryin'. She cry until now, this mornin'. She be ver', ver' seek.

"We wait for the car to take the bodies to mortuary, the black moira. They send a telegram to the other wife in Zululand to come."

"And then??"

"The othah wife must go to Post Office to get telegram. Someone will tell her."

Elizabeth finished her tea and got up to put away our tea things. "I gotta wurk, Miz Betty. Thanks for the tea 'n biscuits. It my lunch."

I sadly commiserated with her about her friend, as we exchanged the often-used tones and words of grief that are commonplace here in this violent country "O-o-w, ah-hh...oh-h."

ELIZABETH'S HIGH SPIRITS

Elizabeth arrived to clean our flat in high spirits, literally. As we settled down for our morning tea, I got a strong whiff of the wine she had been sampling in Katie's flat down the corridor. I watched her, garrulous and uncommonly cheery, as she added three heaping spoonfuls of sugar to her tea and then stirred it briskly.

Elizabeth sipped it, paused looking thoughtful, then offhandedly asked, "Miz Betty, you still take pitchers of peepul 'round heah?"

"Why yes, Elizabeth. Would you like me to take yours now?"

"Yas'um. I dun think it ovah. I saw you take Josiah and Petah's pitcher. Now me," she said firmly. She had remembered that when we first arrived in our flat in Braamfontein, I had offered to take a photograph of anyone working there and give them a copy. Over the following weeks, several of the staff had arrived bringing a favorite treasure so that they would have a visual memento.

But Elizabeth was the main person that I had wanted to know better because I hoped she would be an ongoing contact over the years. Having negatives would reinforce my journal notes and help me remember details. Elizabeth however, had simply ignored my offer of taking her photograph.

When pressed on this point in the past she only replied, with peasant-like suspicion, "Nope."

Evidently it had taken an uncommon amount of Katie's favorite wine for Elizabeth to decide to have her picture taken now.

"Where would you like to sit?" I asked, looking around the small living room portion of our flat that we called the visitor's area. It consisted of four bamboo chairs and a small coffee table.

"Oh, not here," she said hastily, eyeing the two large desks, filing cabinets and bookcases that dominated our living room, "Le's go to Katie's flat. It's *purty*."

I reluctantly followed her down to the end of the hall and waited as she unlocked the door with her cleaner's key. I felt guilty and somewhat anxious about being inside Katie's flat illegally. I didn't even know her except through Elizabeth's description. How could I explain my presence if she unexpectedly returned? Or what if our strict flat manager, Mrs. Wood, came along looking for Elizabeth?

As we walked in I looked around and had to agree that Katie's place *was* certainly prettier than ours with her flowered drapes, leather-covered bar stools, and easy chairs.

I checked the available lighting with my camera meter near an easy chair. But Elizabeth had already hoisted her ample self onto a bar stool, crossed her legs with difficulty and posed with an elegant crystal wine goblet held aloft.

"You c'n take my pichur now," she said, looking at me with a big smile on her round, moon face. For 30 seconds, she was royalty. I was certain it would make a fine picture.

FIELD WORK PHOTOS

Professor Hammond-Tooke leaned forward in his leather chair to empty his pipe in the commodious ashtray that sat on his desk. It was another of our two-hour sessions that he arranged for me twice a month over the ten years he was my thesis supervisor. During our sessions, he always told his secretary not to disturb us except for bringing tea. His large, handsome office was filled with books, a respectable number of them he himself had authored, which always intimidated me as I wrestled with my own thesis.

I had reached an impasse in analyzing my data, and I needed a suggestion on how to evaluate my many slides of Ndebele homesteads to prove my argument that related to the title "Paint, Pride and Politics."

At this point I was overwhelmed with the number of slides I had taken over the three years of fieldwork in the Homelands, and I wasn't sure what to do next. The striking decorations on the Ndebele mud huts had intrigued me for many years. Along with the detailed interviewing that Hilda, my interpreter, and I had conducted over time, taking the slides had been an important part of my methodology. However, my supervisor at this juncture said it was important to use them to display the strong stylistic differences that had emerged among the different tribal groups in the Transvaal Province.

"One can only procrastinate a certain length of time until, inevitably, you have to prove your point and begin writing," he pointed out.

"Compare and contrast," he advised. "Spread the slides out and visually evaluate what the differences are."

He again filled his pipe and suggested, "Go home and really analyze what you have."

With that he concluded our session, and I had to face the next hurdle in the analysis.

With troubled thoughts, I left the university and went home, determined to conquer the next daunting step. On my dining room table I gathered a large number of slides and spread them out over two light tables to better see them and do some serious thinking.

It was at this point that Elizabeth came in to do her daily flat cleaning.

She looked at my large array of slides and gave a small shout, "Woo woo!"

"Whut you doin' with all them pichurs, Miz Betty?" she said, eyeing the messy table.

"I use them in my work, Elizabeth, so I can't clean off the table until tomorrow."

"Whuffo you take all them pichurs? You make calendars?"

"No, no. It's for my work at the university," I said, not wanting to go into details.

"The univuh-sity? They pay you lotsa money for 'em?" she asked, looking at the enormous number of slides.

"Um-m, well, no. I have to pay for them myself. In fact," thinking of the irony, "I pay the university to be able to do this."

By then I began feeling somewhat sorry for myself about the cost of the higher degree I was tackling.

"You pay *them*?" Elizabeth asked in disbelief. "Whuffo you do that?"

"Well, it's part of what I have to do." I replied lamely.

But privately her remark about making calendars triggered a thought: *Why not sell some of these to a calendar company and get some money to help with the costs?*

When I looked up the number of the South Africa Today calendar company and phoned them, they said delightedly, "You have pictures of your field work among the Ndebele?"

"Yes, and I was wondering if you would be interested in buying any of my slides for next year's calendar?"

"Indeed we would. It's really much more interesting for us

to have some pictures of the tribal people in the Homelands, but not many of our photographers have the government permit that allows them to be out there. Do please send us some. and we'll be happy to pay you for any that we use."

So, thanks to Elizabeth, thus began a fruitful moonlighting operation I was able to arrange with the South Africa Today calendar company that actually did end up helping pay for a good portion of my photography costs from then on.

HARSH LESSONS

My contribution to our family finances were never large or steady, but Jack had borne up well under this omission. My work record showed a spotty career of improvising jobs and being a perpetual student, which instead *cost* Jack money.

A temp job on a British film crew provided an opportunity to make a contribution. So upon returning to Johannesburg from Botswana to film their independence from Britain, I proudly showed Jack my British cashier's check of 250 pounds sterling. I was a bit disappointed when he asked diffidently, "OK. What would you like to do with it?"

After a discussion we decided to mail it to my parents in Oregon because an extra few hundred dollars would be a pleasant surprise. We mailed it, and I promptly forgot about it.

A week later the phone rang in our flat. When I answered, I was disturbed to hear, slowly and distinctly in a heavy Afrikaans accent, "I vant to speak to John Schneider," a man demanded loudly.

"He's not here now. What is it you want?"

"This is Lt. Estehuezen at John Vorster Square. He's to report here tomorrow morning, first thing," he said brusquely.

My heart sank. I found my hands shaking as I hung up the phone. John Vorster Square was the infamous headquarters of the South African Police.

The newspapers periodically gave reports of prisoners or suspects "falling" out of the high windows after long, arduous questioning, and dying on the pavement below. Torture was not unknown. Other veiled reports were about prisoners who "slipped on the soap in the shower" and died.

"Miz Betty, whaffo you look so scared?" Elizabeth asked,

worriedly.

"Jack has to report to John Vorster Square," I replied shakily, "Tomorrow! I can't let him go alone."

"Oh, Miz Betty, you-all goin' to prison? Thas' a terrible place, John Vorster Square. People nevah come back from there. I'm goin' down on my knees right now, an' pray fer you," she cried -- and did.

Shaken, I decided to call the American Consul General's office. "Two American citizens have been called down to John Vorster Square, and I think you should know," I said worriedly.

After a few cursory inquiries, the diplomat sighed heavily, "Well, keep us informed," and hung up.

No help there.

Next day, when Jack and I arrived at the tall, blue building housing the notorious South African Police headquarters we were sent up to Lt. Estehuezen's office on the seventh floor. We took the lift. Later, walking along the long hall, I couldn't help noticing through the open doors that many of the men had headphones on. Tapping phone conversations, we surmised. Others were examining stacks of opened letters. Suddenly that explained to me the several blank windowed envelopes that had properly arrived in our mailbox earlier, although our address was folded inside.

It was a very busy place. I wondered what would happen if we never returned to our flat from this building. I tried to comfort myself by thinking that at least the political officer in the American Consul's office knew where we were.

We finally located Lt. Estehuezen's office. We waited outside his office a long time. He was just completing the grilling of a young hippie couple that had been picked up coming across the Zimbabwe/South African border. After their questioning, they left in tears, and the lieutenant motioned for us to come inside.

We waited nervously. I noted ironically, that as many Afrikaans men are, he was large-boned, blond and good-looking. He said nothing for a long time, but rifled through the stacks of opened letters on his desk, sometimes snorting while removing a sheet of aluminum paper or wax paper inside an envelope. Evidently these were devices the sender hoped would outwit the scanning machine.

Still we waited.

Suddenly, the lieutenant snatched one of the opened envelopes and waved it in Jack's face, shouting, "This yours?"

Jack carefully looked at the envelope addressed to my parents in Oregon, then said angrily, "Yes! And what are you doing with it?" Concerned, I kicked him under the table. If I lost my government permit to do fieldwork in the Homelands, I wouldn't be able to finish my thesis.

Lt. Estehuezen smiled grimly, "What am I doing with it?" He paused, "Well, that's for *me* to know, and *you* to find out," he retorted with ill-concealed satisfaction. It took awhile for us to figure out what we had done wrong because he never gave any facts or actually explained. From the range of his questions and accusations he threw at us, we gradually realized what the charges were.

Apparently the currency laws in South Africa are far-reaching. I had known we could never travel overseas without getting the South African government's stamp of approval in our passport for the R1,000 limit — no matter how distant the travel, nor how long the vacation — and approval was not easily granted. Now we were learning that no South African citizen could send money outside without government approval. As South African permanent residents, we were subject to the same law. Not knowing the details of the law was no excuse. According to South African law during the National Emergency in the 1970s and 1980s, if charged, you were considered guilty until you could prove your innocence. You could be held, detained and questioned for an unlimited time. Habeas corpus existed in American law, but not in South African law at that time.

I spoke up. "That money is mine. My husband had nothing to do with it."

"Likely story," scoffed the lieutenant, "And just what did

you have to do with it?"

"I was free-lancing with UPI-TV News, covering Botswana's independence anniversary celebration. That cashier's check was my pay."

"A cashier's check made out to a Peter Snow?" he sneered.

With that, I told him about free-lancing with UPI-TV News and the circumstances of that particular check, but his skepticism increased. With ill-concealed impatience he pointed out the police knew I was enrolled at the university (which he thought was highly suspect as well). Evidently our phone was tapped, as we had long suspected.

"And what is a woman in her fifties doing in university?" he asked, combining contempt with disbelief. A mature foreign student, especially a woman, was a rare species in apartheid South Africa.

Then, turning to my husband, he suddenly pulled his gun from its holster and began waving it in circles over his head, shouting, "You foreigners make me sick. Coming here to feather your nest, working at the university, then leaving when the going gets tough."

Which triggered Jack's indignant response, "Feather our nest? Do you know what a senior lecturer earns here?" Again I kicked him hard under the table.

Lt. Estehuezen laid his gun on his desk. Jack and I sat opposite him, visibly shaken by this furious display. Then he slowly and deliberately removed the bullets one by one, set them on end, looked at them thoughtfully, then carefully reinserted them. After a long pause, he said,

"Well, I won't need Mr. Schneider any more, but you," he said, looking at me, with another pause to let it sink in, "will return Monday morning to answer some questions."

We got up to leave. I was extremely upset and close to hysterics, hardly understanding that we had been dismissed. But Jack took my arm and grimly helped me walk out.

My weekend was a total loss. I suddenly realized what other students and faculty had been going through. A number of them were already in prison. My close faculty friend in anthropology, David Webster, had been having tea parties where those of us invited were to bring textbooks. David could then deliver the textbooks to the students on visitor's day so they could keep up with their classes while they were in prison. We all hoped they would not be too far behind when they were finally released. Later we learned that David was murdered for that.

But that had been last week. The coming week I had an urgent appointment with Lt. Estehuezen. I knew that I had better prepare myself as best I could.

The following Monday morning Lt. Estehuezen perfunctorily acknowledged me at his office, leaning back in his chair with a superior smile. With relish, he began a series of intermittent questioning.

"Why," he quizzed me sarcastically, "did you try to deliberately defraud the South African government's currency law by sending money to the States? Did you think you could get by without anyone knowing?"

"What else have you been sending out to them?" he said, his voice rising.

"I suppose now you'll tell me that you can take any amount of money out of this country whenever you travel, that it?" he shouted, while pounding his desk.

"I'll have you know we have currency laws here. You are expected to know that." Pause.

"By the way, bring your passport in here tomorrow. I intend to see if you've been traveling back to the States taking lots of our currency with you and then returning with lots of your U.S. currency.

"You foreigners think you are so clever that we'd never suspect what is going on."

He leaned closer in an intimate fashion, saying in a quietly ominous tone, "But you're not getting away with it anymore, you hear? I'll see to that."

Then he suddenly stood up, shaking his fist and shouted, "I hate you academics with your superior attitude!"

"What were you doing getting involved with British

television news? Who is this Peter Snow?" he continued in an insinuating tone, "and why did he give the check to *you*?"

The questions came so fast, there was no time to answer, even if I had wanted to. As I left the police lieutenant's office badly shaken, I walked back to my car. In the distance, atop a tall building where the American Consul had an office, the American flag flying above it fluttered in the breeze. I found tears running down my cheeks.

The ordeal lasted several interminable weeks. During apartheid, the South African police were usually belligerent with foreigners, especially foreign journalists, assuming they were agent provocateurs stirring the blacks up to revolt. It was difficult for journalists or any media person to even get a visa unless they disguised their profession by identifying themselves as an ESL teacher (English as a second language) or a foreign aid worker. Some of their job descriptions were quite creative, usually having to do with word-smithing.

The lieutenant scoffed at the idea of my student status. He was artful. He would sometimes stop the bullying and shouting and suddenly get friendly. Once he cunningly leaned closer and murmured companionably, "I once went back to university, but realized that was a stupid way to try to get ahead." Then suddenly, without warning, he turned on me, saying, "I don't believe you, saying you are a student. Not at your age. What are you really doing? We know you're spying."

"I was only…." I said haltingly.

As I tried to explain my temporary overseas press work, he interrupted, saying quietly yet ominously,

"Just sign this paper, and I'll let you go with no more questions."

Terrified, I refused. I was not about to sign anything. Another time, pounding the desk, he threatened me saying, "You're going to sign it to finish this thing, and then you'll have a police record with fingerprints for the rest of your life."

That paper spelled out that I was well aware of trying to avoid the South African currency law by secreting money in a message to the United States, which of course I hadn't done.

I was truly upset. I finally hired a knowledgeable lawyer to help me handle the situation. Unfortunately he was of little help because most of his time was taken up with other university people who were already in jail for anti-apartheid activities and badly needed his expertise.

Three weeks into this daily interrogation, one Friday evening our good friend Raymond Jaffe phoned to invite us to dinner at his home with his wife.

Jack answered saying, "We'd love to, Raymond, but I'm afraid we can't because Betty is having hysterics." Lt. Estehuezen had informed me earlier that day that on Monday he was going to book me.

"What's the trouble?" asked Raymond.

Jack handed me the phone. I tried to explain what was going on, while Raymond listened carefully. Belatedly, I realized Raymond was a Queen's Counselor, the highest ranking that existed for an attorney in South Africa.

"Betty, would you be willing to talk to the public prosecutor on Monday afternoon and tell him exactly what happened?" asked Raymond.

"Yes," I sobbed.

"So come tonight, have dinner with us and enjoy yourself," he counseled.

Monday morning, very early, Raymond called me to tell me to go to Lt. Esteheuzen's office to pick up my check.

"It's again yours," Raymond assured me.

Flabbergasted, I asked him, "What happened?"

"Well, the public prosecutor pointed out to the lieutenant that if Mrs. Schneider were intending to defraud the government's law on currency exchange, she surely wouldn't have put her return address on the envelope."

Case dismissed.

ELIZABETH'S STAY IN HOSPITAL

"Ah, Elizabeth, you're back! I've missed you," I said. "I hope everything is all right at home."

"No'm. I'se been seek, real seek," she said, sitting down on a chair with a deep sigh. But I'se gotta wurk. They no pay me if m'wurk don' get done."

"Oh, I'm so sorry," I said, truly disturbed. She was obviously still in pain, and I wanted to help in any way I could. She had not been at work for three days, so I knew she must have been really ill. She didn't miss working if she could help it because that meant she wouldn't get paid, and the many people whom she supported would suffer.

"I had such a bad hurt in m' back an' chest, n' all aroun' that Tuesday night I hadda ask my boy David t'get 'n ambulance to take me to Bara," she said. "It cost me R2.50 fur th' ride, so 'spensive. They put me inna chaiah in the hospital, an' I sat fer a long time. My legs they swelled up because theah was no place to be but that chaiah. The doctahs they come an' they jus' look," she shrugged. "an' then they go fer tea. They go fer a long time, 'n mebbe they don' come back."

"Elizabeth, were there enough doctors out there in Baragwaneth?" Baragwaneth was the one black hospital in Soweto, aside from the Eye Hospital. The Eye Hospital treated the pervasive eye diseases including the river blindness that plagued the black population living near the river, which was heavily infested with flies. The people used the river to bathe if they didn't have a water spigot near their home.

"*Yebo*," Elizabeth said. "Plenty doctahs theah in Bara, but they jus' don' care. I think they see so much, they jus' don' care anymore, so they go away. "One woman, she come from long, long away, out theah," Elizabeth pointed in a generally southwest direction. "She bring her ole man. She is sick, she so sick he nevah open his eyes. I went to look. The ole man she waits. She waits fer a long time. Th' doctah he come an' he jus' bend ovah an' he look at his eyes. They not open. They don' open. Th' doctah, he jus' walk away like this," she said, tossing her head and imitating the doctor's shrug.

"Th' beds are so full, too much full. No place t' sleep. It come night, an' I sleep on th' bench. They bring me two blankets It's *cold*. I sleep on th' bench Tuesday and Wednesday night. It's too cold! "Th' doctah, he look at me in th' day. In the day sometimes th' doctah will look at you, but not at night. They not theah at night. In the day he took m' temp-ture. He tell me I mus' stay there five days. I say, 'Please, doctah, give me m' discharge so I c'n maybe go back to wurk. I'se afraid I lose my job. I want t' go home where it's warm an' I c'n get somethin' to eat.' The doctah, he give me a shot," Elizabeth said, imitating a jab in her upper arm, "an' he write a lettah to Miz Wood so I c'n go to the clinic an' not lose m' job."Th' food it's so little. Fer breakfast I got tea 'n bread. Th' lunch, a little bit of meat," Elizabeth illustrated with two circles of her fingers, " 'bout two spoons, an' some mealies.

"So many peepul sick, real sick. Th' childern, ever where they are, they die like this. She made a throw-away motion of her arms before concluding, "Many, many die."

"It bettah to be at home. I don' like hospital. No one take notice of you theah. Sometime in th' day they do, but at night, nevah. Th' beds they too full. Today, befoah I come to wurk, they take my temp'ture at th' hospital and then I come to wurk with a letter fer Miz Wood. I'll try to wurk. My back an' inside (indicating chest and back area) they hurt so much." She gently coughed, obviously in pain.

While having our tea and rusks, she seemed very hungry, so I gave her four helpings of rusks to eat with her tea. She had three cups of tea with milk and white sugar.

I fervently wished she would let me give her more food, but she was too proud and wouldn't.

AIRPLANES

As we slowly got to know each other over our daily milk-tea, we exchanged little culture capsules. Elizabeth shared vignettes about her life in Soweto, with its ups and downs, and quizzed me thoroughly about my life. She knew nothing about America and kept saying we must be from England where King George was from, except that we "talked funny, not like the others."

But then, one day when our visitors, son Jonathan and wife Kristan, were leaving to return to the States, Elizabeth became more curious about that world. As she eyed their two small bags, she said knowingly, but still questioningly, "They pay extra for each bundle?"

That reminded me that on homeland buses, the blacks pay an extra fee for each package, including chickens and goats.

I replied, "No, the fare from America is expensive, so they don't charge extra for bags."

Elizabeth asked, "What they chahge?"

"Well, about 1,200 rand," I said, which caused her to shout, "Oooo, woo, woo," a common response of Africans to a surprising fact.

After a long pause she asked, "What they do up there (pointing skyward) in the plane when the sky she's closed down??"

So I started to explain, "Well, above the clouds it's bright and sunny."

Elizabeth looked skeptical, but continued her questions. "An' how the pilot go through up there when it's *dahk*?" My layman's description of radio navigation had to suffice, and I went on to explain a layer of clouds between us and the sun. The plane flies up through it, bumpy at times, but it's smooth up above, "but their seat belts are fastened," I reassured her.

Elizabeth queried in amazement, "Then they can't move around when they go t' Ametica?"

I explained, "Oh yes, after they are high enough. They can get up and walk around some."

"Have they little beds to sleep in up there?" she asked, extremely curious now.

I responded, "No, only small pillows and a blanket, and they lean back in their comfortable chairs. It takes a long time to go to America, something like 24 hours. They sleep, they eat, they go to the loo."

"How they eat?" she asked.

"Well, there is a little kitchen, and attendants heat the meals and bring them to your seat. Your table is a little tray on the back of the seat ahead."

"Ow-w-w, a stove up there! No wonder they chahge so much." Pause. "C'n they drive their car up there? Can they drive their car to Ametica?"

"No, it's too far, and there's a lot of water in between, an ocean or two, but you can send your car by ship." That is how our car came, and she knows that with its left-hand drive it's different from cars here.

Longer pause. "That's heavy to go so long." She stirred sugar into her tea and reached for a biscuit.

I reassured her "There are books, magazines to read, a movie, er bioscope," as they said in South Africa.

"A bioscope? How they do that?"

I tried a complicated explanation of how everyone can see the movie, but only those who buy earphones could hear it (in those days). These finer points were lost on Elizabeth. She was still in a daze about a bioscope and a stove.

Elizabeth then asked, "When they get to Ametica, how they get *down*?

I gave a simple explanation about how some men in a tower down there direct all the planes in the sky, and they tell each pilot to take his turn in coming down. (Which is about all I knew about air controllers.)

"Some day, I want to see inside that plane. How's it look?"

"Well, there's a corridor down the center, and the seats are on each side."

"Can they peek out the window and see down there even when they's tied down? she asked, pointing down.

"Yes, there are windows on each side, and there are cupboards above for some of your luggage."

Elizabeth said, shaking her head, "I come to see a plane inside some day, just when it's on th' ground. I want t' see this thing."

Three days later, Elizabeth knocked at the door.

"They back there now? That Ametica?"

I nodded, and she shook her head in amazement.

"I tell the gulls in the lift. My madam she tell me all about the air-eo-plane with bioscope inside and the stove and loo, and they say to me, "Your madam, she nice to tell you all these things."

With that, Elizabeth left, beaming her big, broad smile.

ELIZABETH AND KING GEORGE

Elizabeth and I were sitting at the kitchen part of the snack bar having our daily tea. The snack bar in our flat was ingeniously placed between the kitchen and the living room. On the kitchen side it was low, so one could sit in a normal chair when drinking tea. The living room side was high, so one had to sit on a high stool to drink tea comfortably. We usually settled on the kitchen side, closer to the warm stove and teakettle. It got cold in winter, with frequent frost due to Johannesburg's high altitude.

This day, during our 11 a.m. tea break, Elizabeth was sitting there thoughtfully reminiscing as she stirred her fourth spoonful of sugar into her cup. She sighed after sipping her strong tea and milk and then remarked, "Things were much bettah when we had King George," she said. "I 'membah when I wuz in school, we paid nothin' t' go t' school."

I mentally calculated the date easily because we were born about the same year. If she went to school for two years at ages 6 to 8, it was probably from 1928 to 1930, long before 1948 when the Nationalist Party of the Afrikaners replaced the English government.

As she was talking about King George, I suddenly realized that now pupils ("scholars," as they were called) had to pay for public school in Soweto. In contrast, if white children went to their public schools in Johannesburg, there was no charge, but most of the white children went to private schools.

Elizabeth continued, while adding another spoonful of sugar, "Th' exercises were from th' school (writing notebooks were called exercise books). Th' school gave 'em. Now they give nothin'."

She reminisced, looking off into space, "An' we had food,

good food, always in th' mornin' hot choc'late in th' cold weather an' two slices of bread. Then butter on it or marmalade or even peanut butter. At noon we always got a big glass o' milk like this," she said, indicating a tall glass by holding one hand horizontally above the table.

"And then we had fruit. Whatevah it was, app-lees or nex' day we got dried peaches or grapes. We could take four app-lees, then still come back the next day fer food. It was good then, befoah King George died," she sighed. "Now th' Afrikaner give nothin'. My childern, they get nothin' at school. An' we pay at school fer books, too, an' the exercises. The exercises are '*spensive* now.

"King George from England was a good man. It never bin good since he died. Th' Afrikaner changed it all," she said wistfully.

"My childern they get nothin'. No food. But when I wuz in school it were differ'nt."

"Thank you for the tea an' bread, madam. It's m' lunch. I only eat two times a day."

She tidied up the kitchen, washed the cups and saucers, and put away the tea canister, sugar and the anise-flavored rusks until tomorrow.

BANKING WITH ELIZABETH

"Elizabeth, I have to go to the bank and get some money for next week's field trip" I said, watching worriedly as she happily finished ironing Jack's shirt with an appallingly hot iron as usual. *That shirt would never drip-dry wrinkle-free again,* my mind fretted.

"The bank? Whuffo you get money from bank? You wuhk there?" she questioned.

"No, no. That's where we hold our money and take some out each week as we need it. See, the university sends Jack's salary to the bank instead of giving it to us. It's safer that way."

"Why not bring it home to use it? That's quicker," Elizabeth reasoned.

I paused. This new domain needed an explanation. Maybe I could help her avoid the *tsotsis*, the South African street thugs armed with knives who waylayed workers on payday.

"Well, this way it's safer. I don't have to pick it up, and it earns a bit of money," I explained.

"How come it earn money, and you do nuthin'?" she asked.

"Varsity transfers Jack's salary into the bank to hold, and the part we don't use right away earns interest."

"What means interest?" she queried.

"That's the money the bank adds so you get more than you put in." But Elizabeth looked skeptical. Obviously this path into higher finance was doomed, so I decided to approach it another way.

"Elizabeth, if you put your extra money into your own bank account, you can watch it grow. You won't have to worry about the *tsotsis* stealing it. Let's open your own account at Nedbank, and you'll see."

"Hm-m. Sounds like fishy to me, but OK," Elizabeth reluctantly agreed. "I don' like them riffy-raff *tsotsis*."

"Right! We'll get an application and bring it back for you to fill out."

We sneaked out of our building when no one was looking, since Elizabeth was supposed to be working, and walked the short distance from our flat to Nedbank. I asked the bank clerk for an application to open an account, usually a source of delight to American bank clerks, while indicating it was for my cleaning woman.

The Afrikaans woman clerk, eyeing Elizabeth skeptically said, "She can't do it unless she's literate, and most aren't. She has to be able to write her name. Can *she*?"

Elizabeth looked out into space, embarrassed by the clerk's scorn.

"No problem" I assured her outwardly, stung by the clerk's attitude, but inside I worried as I picked up two applications in case she was right.

When we got home, I placed her application on the table and explained to Elizabeth she need only sign her name, and I would finish the form for her.

With ceremony Elizabeth settled her ample frame in a chair and centered the application in front of her. At that point she reached into her bosom to retrieve her identity passbook that she opened in front of her. She readjusted her seat, moved the application more precisely into place and fiercely grabbed the pen. For ten minutes she carefully and slowly copied each letter of her identity passbook name onto the form, heaving a great sigh when she finished. In checking it, I saw her 'Elizabeth' was shakily, but correctly penned; however, her surname, Mngadi, was spelled Mngati. There might be some problem here…

"Elizabeth, that's fine," I complimented her, "except we better replace the 't' with a 'd' in your *isibongo,* (surname); that's the way the passbook spells it."

"No difference," she said. I cautiously agreed, knowing enough Zulu by now that the pronunciation could account for the difference. But that clerk wouldn't know it, and the pace of Elizabeth writing her name would certainly cause comment.

"Let's practice each day for a week so you can do it a little faster; then we'll go to Nedbank together," I suggested.

Elizabeth worriedly agreed and the following week, each day after tea, she dutifully repeated the entire signing ceremony, including copying the passbook version of her name. The time lessened. However, I gave up on the t/d substitution.

When next we arrived at Nedbank, located a few blocks beyond our flat building, there the dour clerk was, waiting. I planned to give the bank a signed, completed application, thus hoping to forestall a visible, lengthy test of the signing.

"Here is the application for Elizabeth's new account," I said.

The clerk said nothing but she scrutinized the signature for a long time. Next to me, Elizabeth's worried frown, which often appeared when dealing with arrogant white people, began creasing her wide face, and she quietly stepped behind me.

"Very well" said the clerk. "If you will guarantee this and pick up her statement each month, she can open an account," and so we opened her bank account.

On the way home Elizabeth confided that she didn't have extra money to bank. She spent everything almost the day she earned it. She had to buy candles, the coal to cook with, the mealie-meal to eat and her train ticket to get to work. The rent had to be paid, and there were the children's school uniforms.

"But thank you for showing me the bank" she said courteously as we returned to our flat for afternoon tea.

I then decided the best interest Elizabeth could earn would be to raise her income, still using cash for the extra work she did for me. Jack's and my plan to quietly increase Elizabeth's earnings by adding to her bank account would be too complicated for her to manage.

THE NEIGHBORS' DRINKING

Sighing, Elizabeth sat down, slipping off the comfortable bedroom slippers she substituted for shoes when her feet and legs were as swollen as they were today. She reached for the sugar bowl to enrich her pungent Five Roses tea with five spoonfuls. She loved sugar, even more than the anise seed rusks we shared at our morning respite. Today was a Friday. We had lived here awhile, but Elizabeth felt that I, as a relative newcomer, should know more about my neighbors on the seventh floor.

"That man he live nex' doah? He a good man, but he don' want *nobody* in her flat." (Elizabeth was still having trouble with "his" and "her.") "But he give me shoes for my son, David. My David, he sick in the head," she added matter-of-factly describing her mentally impaired son.

She continued, "Tha' man, she's nice, but no one can come into his flat," referring to the solitary Hungarian draftsman who lived there.

I nodded knowingly. This neighbor had never spoken to me.

Elizabeth, noticing the sun was going behind a cloud complained, "Look, she's closin' down. Now it's Friday 'n she close down," she added fretfully.

Her big concern was getting her wash done on weekends in Soweto. With no sun, clothes would not dry. She stirred more milk and sugar into her second cup of tea and continued.

"You know Katie in th' front flat?" she continued the roster and proceeded with the neighborhood gossip. "She drink so much. Now it's Friday an' so Katie and her frien's in 201 and 203 come up an' drink. They have big bottles of the hot stuff, Bols Brandy, *real hot!* They drink that, and gin." Her eyebrows went up.

"It no good to drink befoah married. Who gonna marry a drinkin' woman? Bettah to get married furst, *then* drink. Not so much trouble." she philosophized. "One lady ovah in Petty's Scott," the nearby Paris Court block of flats, "she drink. Her husban' get tired. One day he took all her clothes an' send them away. Then he take the childern and went back to that othah country, Rhodesia. He get tired of her always drinkin' all day," Elizabeth nodded knowingly.

She continued, "Tonight Katie and her two frien's come in togethah in her flat, and they drink, much. They not so bad. They not shout and run aroun.' They're jus' quiet an' drink. But tomorra when I come t' her flat, it's all mixed up. Things heah an' things ovah theah. I gotta straighten the mixed-up things…glasses all aroun.'

"Ovah in Petty's Scott it's *wurse* than heah. This flat she quiet on Fridays and Satidays, but ovah theah, when you look ovah from the 11th floah at night, you can see 'em all runnin' aroun'. Those people, those blacks, and gulls, they all dancin' and singin' in the corridahs. They drink an' shout. It's tettible. Not so bad as in Hillbrow, thass wurse. They run past youah door in th' flat. They hit people ovah the head with bottles, but heah, this's good. Upstaahs, Josiah and Petah," meaning the night watchman and furnace boy, "they drink up theah, but not bad stuff. Bantu beer they buy at the stoah. They sit quiet in theah rooms on the 14th."

"In Petty's Scott, two men they walk intah th' room wheah the night watchman sleep on th' bed. They take out a gun and shoot him dead. Tha' was last year, d'you remembah?"

I shook my head. Gossip about nearby flat staff hadn't gotten this far.

"Miz Wood," our aging manager, "she drink on a day like this." It was cloudy, overcast. "By 11 o'clock she staht to drink. Not too much, but she drink. Then about 3, she staht shoutin' at everbuddy and walk up and down the sta-ahs. 'Josiah, wheah are you? Nothin' is done heah. Come down heah.' She scream at everbuddy," Elizabeth continued.

"When I heah her walk up an' down the staahs, ah close th' doah like this." She gently pushed my upstanding breadboard against the wall to demonstrate. "I not want her to see me. If you in the corridor she come along and she see one leetle stick on th' ground, then she shout, 'Look at this on the floah! No one is workin' 'less I tell 'em. I don' think this corridah's been cleaned for three days. Lookit this stick! Elizabeth, come sweep it up!'

"The only thing to do is to take yoah broom and say, 'yez, Miz Wood' 'cause she not listen to anythin'. You take yoah broom and start wurkin' at the stick while she look even though it is not time to clean the corridahs." She explained righteously, "It's only 11 o'clock, and those we clean at 3, but bettah to jus' take th' broom, an' when she walk away, just put yoah broom away. Miz Wood, she not bad to drink, just a leetle bit. But when she drink, she shout. When you heah her shout, you know she been drinkin'.

"But Miz Wood's nice. I don' wan' her to die. She's good. Only she drink a leetle bit and she shout."

And just then we heard Mrs. Wood yell for Elizabeth, so we hastily finished our tea. Elizabeth sighed. Our tea with insider information about my neighbors was finished.

I retired to my desk so Mrs. Wood wouldn't know we had been having a tea break together. Those colonials had strong feelings about the proper interaction between madam and maid. Elizabeth got up with effort to open the front door to say, "Yez, Miz Wood?"

Her swollen legs and feet were bothering her a lot that day.

SWEETIE BUSINESS

Elizabeth and I had come to trust and rely on one another. During our morning tea one day, Elizabeth told me she had been mulling over how she could take advantage of the convenient location of her house to earn some money.

"If I could sell some sweeties in front of m'house," she said, "I cud make lotsa money. M'house, she's on th' way to th' train an' the taxi stand. Ever' day ever'buddy walk past my house to get to th' train to Joburg. If I put my li'l table there with sweeties in front of m'house, they all gonna buy some when they walk past. Ever'one like sweeties," she said.

Having noticed the girth of many black women, including Elizabeth, I saw her point.

"It too hard fer me to get to factory to buy so much sweeties and carry 'em on th' train," she said. "They'd be stolen by riffy-raff; y'know, *tsotsis*," using her description of the thieves that roamed the commuter trains. "An' besides them factory white peepul won't believe me to have s' much money," she concluded.

I noted this comment in my journal that day. Later, when my American friend Barbara saw it and heard about Elizabeth's business plan, she excitedly offered to contribute a R250 startup fund if I would organize the rest of it.

My job would be to smuggle Elizabeth out of the flat and into my car and then find the wholesale candy factory. After that, with Elizabeth's whispered guidance at the factory she could point out which candy bundles would sell the best, and I would be the front woman for the purchase.

It would be complicated, but I thought we could try it.

Meanwhile, Elizabeth, stirring her tea at my kitchen table and musing over her problem said wistfully, "If I only had money to buy lotsa sweeties, I cud get really, really rich!"

Then I had a thought. "Who would sit at that little table in Jabulani when you're at work here in Johannesburg?" I asked.

"Oh, lotsa people live at m'house and they c'n wuhk when I'm not theah," Elizabeth said.

"But it too hard to get to factory to buy so much sweeties and carry 'em on train," she sighed resignedly, putting away our tea things and getting on with her work.

"Let's try it," I said impulsively. Elizabeth's surprised face suddenly beamed like a beacon.

"Yassum, Miz Betty, I'se game."

And so we did it, and that was the beginning of our venture fund that would support Elizabeth's entrepreneurial start-up.

When she furtively returned to our flat later to carry out the scheme, we put our regular escape plan into action.

We got out of the flat safely and downstairs to the garage without the manager Mrs. Wood or Josiah, the building watchman, seeing us. As usual, plump Elizabeth crouched on the back floor of my little BMW with difficulty as we drove out of the garage. A few blocks later, I let her out to get into the front seat with me, as we always did. I checked my map to the location of the factory and we then began the drive there to put our plan into action.

It was many miles outside of town, but when we finally arrived, I saw it was an enormous factory. As we looked around, I discovered it had a section for wholesale customers.

"Who-o-o-ee!" exclaimed Elizabeth, looking around as we got out of the car and walked into the large wholesale section.

We wandered all around the wholesale shop. With her furtive guidance, I bought an extravagant number of candies that Elizabeth had quietly recommended. These were the ones she intended to sort and pack separately at home.

Elizabeth was right because when I finally went to pay, the suspicious wholesale manager frowned and asked, "Are all those candies for you? What do you want so many for?"

"I'm giving a farewell party for my large staff, and we need a good number of candies," I rapidly improvised in my

American accent.

Well, it was a discount candy factory and I had no vendor's permit. Besides, not being Indian, Chinese or black, I didn't look like a typical trading storeowner. I held my breath as I was paying for it, and fortunately I made the large purchase without further problems.

Shopping done, I drove out to Soweto's Jabulani with Elizabeth, who was happily clutching her many bundles of sweeties. We arrived at her home, and when I let her out, we both had an exhilarating feeling of a job well done.

But it was now getting dark and I couldn't help feeling a little nervous as I drove the 15 miles back into Johannesburg from Soweto.

Several weeks later I asked Elizabeth over tea, "How's the sweetie business going?"

"Fine, real good!" she said, her round, shiny face beaming like the sun. "C'n you bring me more sweeties befoah Friday?"

ELIZABETH AND PICASSO

Our good friend Virgilio, who had been one of Jack's teaching assistants during my husband's Fulbright Lectureship in Mozambique, was now living in Portugal. Virgilio, an avid painter who also taught statistics in case he couldn't survive on his painting income, kept in touch with us from Portugal. He was in the middle of trying to exist on his art production when he sent us a colorful postal card with a typical painting of a woman done by Picasso during his Cubist Period. I liked the picture and put it on my refrigerator door.

As Elizabeth finished pouring our tea and went to the fridge to refresh our pitcher of milk, she noticed the postcard of Picasso's painting.

"Funny peeksha here of woman. Who got three legs?" she asked. "Where she live? Why you put crazy peeksha on fridge doah?"

I looked again at the picture postcard. True, the artist had tried to augment the viewer's impression of the woman's anatomy by adding a spare leg, but midst all of the Cubist angles, I thought it was hard to even see that extra leg. However, Virgilio would have loved this rendition of Picasso's work, and I could readily understand why he shared it with us. But to answer Elizabeth's question logically, I was stumped.

"Maybe he had a dream of some woman like that, then thought that he would paint it just to share his idea of it?" I tried to answer her with another question to see where she might go with the topic.

"But Miz Betty, nobuddy look like that! Don' he know any woman so he can *look*?

"Nobuddy dream like that, Miz Betty. That artist mus' be

crazy. Why you want to put it up on the doah?"

"Well, it was done by a famous painter, Picasso, and my friend Virgilio liked it enough to buy it to send to us. We'll put it up for a few days to remind us of him and Picasso and that we should find time to look at art works in a gallery to see what artists are thinking and painting."

"Miz Betty, you need to look at *real* peepul to see how many legs they's got. Thass a bettah idea than jes' looking at someun's funny pitchahs."

Then Elizabeth matter-of-factly put more sugar in her tea, stirred it and reached for an anise seed rusk to dip.

INVITATION TO LUNCH

"Miz Betty," asked Elizabeth carefully, with a worried frown puckering her round face, "You and Mistah Jack come to lunch to my house in Jabulani Sunday?"

"Oh, what a *lovely* invitation, Elizabeth. We'd love to," I said, surprised.

A personal invitation to a white person from someone in black Soweto was a rare and uncommon overture. To have one's *cleaning woman* make the offer was an extraordinary display of trust and affection. I was deeply touched. Curiously, here in Johannesburg, most white madams scarcely knew or even cared in which township their hired staff lived among the satellite constellations collectively called Soweto. I found their indifference to be strange. The typical relationship there between servants and their madams was quite distant, yet, paradoxically, also intimate, in that the servants knew a lot about their madams.

"You and Miz Barbara are good peepul to me, helping me to get my sweetie business." She paused. "D'you think Miz Barbara's family'll come ,too?"

"Oh yes, it would be a thrill for all of them," I assured her.

But privately I worried that Barbara's conservative physics professor husband and her two adolescent children might find this adventure overwhelming and somewhat scary. Going to Soweto was not something many white people did, particularly since the violence there was rapidly increasing. Interactions between whites and blacks could be hazardous.

Nonetheless, I encouraged Elizabeth to invite Barbara. I knew that Barbara, an American, would accept. She felt strongly about supporting black-white interaction, but had little opportunity to get involved. In fact, after reading my journal entries about Elizabeth and morning tea, which she did avidly, she had taken part of the money she inherited from her mother and had invested it in Elizabeth's sweetie business.

After Elizabeth went off to clean other flats, I left a message for Barbara telling about Elizabeth's invitation.

"Yes, Dick will go to Soweto for Elizabeth's lunch. And of course we'll take the children, too," Barbara told me on the phone next day. Her rapid response to Elizabeth's invitation probably did not reflect the heated discussion I imagined she had had with her husband.

Walter, an American, had brought his family to Johannesburg about a year before, not realizing how passionate Barbara would become about the difficult situation of the blacks in South Africa. He tolerated her enthusiasm, but basically was worried about his job. His prestigious post at the university as consultant to the South African government regarding X-ray safety might have been jeopardized by her involvement. Barbara had great energy and would throw herself into situations that she felt were unfair. Also, I was sure upon hearing the word "Soweto" he would be concerned about their safety and that of their children, Linda, nine years old, and Mark, twelve.

When Barbara and Walter had first arrived in South Africa the prior year, she had asked me about how to find a good housekeeper. So I had asked Elizabeth during our morning tea if she knew anyone who would be good. Elizabeth promptly suggested her sister Maria, who was out of work at the time. That arrangement had worked out well.

"Going to Soweto, we'd better go in two cars. I don't think everyone will fit into our little BMW 2002," I said. "I'll lead, and you can follow. Soweto is so big, it's hard to find your way around, and we don't want to get separated."

I had been out to Soweto a few times before, and while I was no expert in finding my way about, in general I felt I could find the way to Elizabeth's house in Jabulani. I, too, was concerned about possible violence, but the lunch would be on a Sunday, and I hoped that many people would be attending their church groups. They might notice white people coming in, but they would be preoccupied. Many religious groups had their gatherings in an empty garage that was officially closed for the weekend, or they would meet under a tree in a part of Soweto that was still free of houses. Or they would meet in someone's house. Visible differences between the various church groups were the vestments they wore and the version of the Bibles they carried. Their beautiful unaccompanied singing and clapping would echo throughout the area. I was looking forward to experiencing Sunday in Soweto.

Finally, transportation for Sunday was settled. We would take two cars.

The next morning, a Friday before our lunch in Soweto, as Elizabeth and I were sharing our elevenses, I said, "We're all looking forward to your lunch Sunday."

"Oh, thass great, Miz Betty," said Elizabeth. "I'se so heppy you can come."

So Elizabeth set about making the arrangements for having six white guests for lunch at her house.

Fourteen people slept or ate at Elizabeth's place in Jabulani. Over the months I'd tried to find out who lived where, how many of them were her own children versus her uncle's, and where exactly they all ate and slept. Living arrangements seemed to change often.

I learned later that they were variously scattered about in several family dwellings: her sister Maria's place, not far away; their recently deceased mother's home nearby; and Elizabeth's place, which actually was a house assigned to her deceased uncle. Elizabeth lived there because, along with her own seven children, she cared for her uncle's four. The government's powerful West Rand Administration Board (WRAB), which monitored who lived where in the various townships, however, did not know these details.

"My Jack is going to kill a goat," Elizabeth said a few days later.

Her roomer Jack was a gold miner from Mozambique who

rented space in Elizabeth's house. He was a Shangaan who had arrived about a year ago from Lourenço Marques, the capital city, where he had a wife and children. Elizabeth's relationship to Jack seemed matter-of-factly-close, probably intimate, I learned from her tea conversations with me. This was not uncommon in a country with South Africa's comparatively good wages, which lured migrant workers from elsewhere. It was often a reciprocal bargain: the man paid rent, helped her with heavier chores and sent home money from his job to his family. On her part, she provided the sleeping space, food and home comforts.

I was curious to get to know Elizabeth's Jack better because she had talked a lot about him.

LUNCH IN SOWETO

After a dust-choking, 15-mile ride into Soweto dodging wild taxis on the dirt roads, we arrived at Elizabeth's house in Jabulani. We parked our cars next to a tall chain link fence along the narrow road in front of her house. We hoped they would be safe.

Elizabeth and her sister Maria greeted us warmly, and their many children swarmed around us, laughing and talking. We met Jack, her roomer, the miner from Mozambique. He was an amiable, muscular man somewhat younger than Elizabeth. As we went into her three-roomed house, Jack started back to the yard where he was cooking pungent chunks of meat in a black iron pot hanging over the fire.

"Ah, *cabrito*," I said sniffing the aroma which reminded me of the Portuguese word for goat from my Mozambican fieldwork days. *Cabrito* was quite tasty. I had eaten it roasted, but never boiled. From the tantalizing smell this would be good, and I relished the thought of *cabrito* for lunch. Elizabeth's Jack, on hearing the word *cabrito*, turned to me and smiled broadly.

As we entered the main room of the small house, my eyes lit upon the kitchen clock that I had given Elizabeth at one time. The clock had been carefully placed inside a plastic bag to protect it from dust and then hung in the place of honor, the living room wall.

The room seemed totally filled with an improvised table, a plywood sheet balanced on the back of a couch and a chest of drawers. It was covered with a freshly ironed bed sheet and set for six people with small bundles of cutlery for each. As the Schneider and Colburn families sat down on the few chairs and several boxes, we all exclaimed over the clever table and how nice it looked. But we were dismayed to hear that Elizabeth, Maria, their children and Elizabeth's Jack would be eating in the kitchen or yard.

"Sit with us! Aren't you going to eat with us?" Barbara and I exclaimed in dismay.

"No, we eat in the kitchen. We must prepare and serve you. *You're the guests*," Elizabeth insisted.

They had no intention of eating with us. The table and cutlery arrangement was for us, the American guests.

I later learned that Elizabeth and Maria had spent the week before borrowing cutlery from their madams for us, "'Cause that's the way you white people eat," Elizabeth explained. As I knew from my fieldwork, the Africans I interviewed ate with their fingers while sitting on the floor, backs against the hut wall and legs straight out.

With much talking and laughing in a mixture of languages, Swazi, English and Zulu, the rest of the household set about dishing up and serving guests first, then all of the family. We had freshly boiled goat meat, with large helpings of mealie-meal. Elizabeth, Maria and the children contentedly worked and ate in the kitchen, much to our disappointment. But the food was excellent, and we were treated to potent Bantu beer, the milky, homemade alcoholic beverage that most Africans drank.

I was reminded of my interpreter Hilda's sideline investigations on our field trips to the villages. She carried her notebook along to gather recipes for the different flavors of Bantu beer, depending upon the grains used in the brewing.

As the others were busily talking, Elizabeth turned and quietly confided to me "I went to the cem-try early this mornin' and brought my Granny heah."

I was startled. Her grandmother had died two months ago.

" We walked slow, and I nevah looked 'round or talked to nobuddy. Thass impotant! We can't f'get ancestors. We must honah them. They watch and take care've us. My Granny don' wan' us to f'get her. I know I mustn't f'get her to come. I poured kaffir beer on her grave befoah we come home heah."

Apparently Elizabeth's enjoyment of lustily singing Methodist hymns at Lesotho Tapia Church on weekends still combined seamlessly with her true animist religion (the worship of ancestors).

"Miz Betty, I got Chris'mas present fer you. I put it in youah car. You need a bench in front of yoah house when you go home to Ametica. My Jack make a seat that I put in yoah car now." With that news, she brought out a small bench, the sort Africans typically sit on outside their front door to watch what's going on in the neighborhood.

Tears suddenly welled up in my eyes. The sun was setting. It was time to leave. As we left Elizabeth's house with everyone shouting goodbye, Jack called out, "ta ta," much to my surprise.

I was startled but pleased. "Ta ta" is a phrase I remembered that everyone in Mozambique always used instead of saying 'goodbye' or '*ciao.*' Suddenly I was very homesick for Lourenco Marques and the good friends we had left there. No South African ever said ta ta.

The sun was low on the horizon. We thanked everyone and got into our cars, still safely parked, for the trip back to Johannesburg. I didn't want to experience driving home from Soweto at night on a weekend, so we left before dark. Most parts of Soweto didn't have electricity, and the roads were not lighted.

Weekends in Soweto and Johannesburg could often turn violent. I still remembered having to take the night watchman from a nearby block of flats one Saturday night to the Emergency Room in Hillbrow after someone smashed a bottle over his head.

GOOD FRIDAY

Elizabeth arrived to do the ironing the day after Good Friday. She was unusually talkative and full of good spirits, literally. She had been up all night celebrating "GO-O-OO-D FRIDA-A-A-Y," as she announced loudly while settling down at the table. Her spoon rattled noisily in the teacup while she energetically stirred the sugar before adding a generous amount of milk. She dipped her rusk into her tea, ate it, then started talking.

"Our chuch sing all night las' night," she said, and from her fuzzy description it sounded like she had been continuing the libations that were used in her all-night singing session so she would be ready for tonight.

I asked, "Can you sleep in tomorrow?"

She shook her head, "No, no, the othah chuch, the sistah chuch, Tapeea, is heah from Pet Reteef," she said, meaning the town named Piet Retief near Swaziland, "and we must nuss 'em. We take good care of 'em, we feed 'em, we sing to 'em. They sing to us. We walk all ovah Soweto," she said as she pulled herself to her feet to demonstrate a jazzy dance step that all black singing groups have. "All night, and we do it again t'night, all night." She collapsed back into her chair, smiling at the memory.

I smiled, too. Churchgoers who didn't have a building or place to worship would find an empty field or gather under a bridge to hold their services. One enthusiastic congregation sometimes met in a large public garage behind our flat. It beautifully amplified their singing.

I wanted to know more about her beliefs. "Elizabeth, what does your church say about Good Friday and Easter?"

"They say theah's a god an' his son he *die* on Friday, then on Sunday, he get *up*," She paused and laughed. "They say that, they say he die 'n get up, like that lady, my frien' I tol' you about las' week. She sat up an' live a few more days, but then she lay down an' die again. I take my friend to th' graveyard today. She dead now, really."

She stirred her tea and reached for an anise seed rusk to dip into her warm milk tea.

"But what do *you* believe? *Really*?" I asked.

"Well, we say we believe that. In chuch we *hafta* say that, or they say we've got th' devil. We devil woman if we don' believe that, so we say we believe." She nodded resignedly, then brightened. "But the real thing is *amaHlozi*. We know the *amaHlozi* is the big thing. Tha's th' *big* one.

"How d'we know whose *amaHlozi* this god is an' his son? With our own *amaHlozi*. We have our Granny. She look after us. She bring us lucky. Our mothah's sistah, our fathah's brothah, our family, our *amaHlodzi* look out fer us.

"We go to th' graveyard. Furst we have tea. We think about 'em 'n we go t' the graveyard an' we talk to 'em. We tell 'em we think about 'em. Then we walk home. You mussn' speak to anyone when you goin' home. Someone say to you, '*Sowbona*, Betty,' you no say nothin' to him. You look straight in front and you walk right home. You go into yoah room and you say to all yoah *amaHlozi,* you say their names, right there, each one, and then they bring you lucky.

"You sprinkle some tea or beer at th' graveyard. It is to them. But the chuch say you muss believe this god and son who die. So we *say* we believe. Othahwise I be devil-woman they say. Ha, ha, ha," she chuckled, and continued her cheery laughter, her ample bosom heaving.

Elizabeth drank some of her tea, but shaking her head at the taste, put three more spoonfuls of sugar in and stirred it hard. She then changed the subject.

"On Sunday at the am-fifi-tee-A-tor [amphitheater]. They have somthin' – I dunno what – but some big thing at am-fifi-tee-A-tor. D'you 'membah that place?"

"Yes," I said, assuming that there had probably been a big Easter celebration there.

I remembered that I had told Elizabeth about going to an African concert at Soweto's amphitheater last week to watch a black band playing intense Zulu music. The wildly enthusiastic crowd danced to the music in the stands as well as out on the field.

Yes, I remembered that place and wanted to share with Elizabeth how exciting it had been and to give her more details about it, but Elizabeth had languidly started to set up the ironing board, and I thought it best to help her. She seemed tired, with her large, swollen legs and her sore feet jammed into her bedroom slippers, but she was happy.

THE BABY

Elizabeth unlocked the front door of our flat with her key and came in quietly. I looked up from my writing to be sure it was she. She usually came in like a fresh wind from the outside, noisily slamming the door, cheerily shouting "Hi," then plunking her cleaning equipment down nearby. There was nothing tip-toe-y about Elizabeth. She knew who she was and what her job required of her, and she would busily set about doing it.

I realized there was no chance of writing on my thesis today. Something was bothering her. Her ragged but freshly washed green uniform was spotless, so whatever bothered her hadn't disrupted her own laundry work at home over the weekend. I thought of how anxious she always was to see that each weekend the sun should be out so she could do her wash, including her uniform. I had earlier thought with irritation, *Why can't the flat management arrange to buy new uniforms once in a while?*

The Bridgeport management had a rule that the uniforms were management property, and they thriftily passed on any unused uniform to a new flat cleaner of similar size. Despite the unvarying green color, the differences in fit made for a motley total effect. No matter that they were worn thin across the bosoms of many flat cleaners of various sizes, no matter they might have been ripped or patched in the back hip region. Even though most were ill fitting, at least they were all green.

"I'se gotta clean under yo-ah stove t'day, Miz Betty. They's things undah there that shouldn' be," she said flatly as she put her cleaning rag on a stick and swished it around under my small kitchen stove.

"Good going, Elizabeth. I've been missing things," I

responded, thinking of Jack's good-natured but awkward willingness to help get meals while I was writing. Elizabeth finished cleaning the kitchen and put the kettle on to boil water for our morning tea. By the time the kettle whistled, she had finished making the bed, and she came in to fix our tea.

As we sat down, I stirred in my milk, and she put five generous spoonfuls of sugar into her tea. By the size of her sugar input, I realized something big was bothering her.

"How's everything going, Elizabeth?" I asked, conversationally.

"I'se so mad! It's not fa-ah [fair]" she muttered, energetically stirring the mound of sugar in her teacup to blend it in.

"What's happened?" I asked.

"Well, y'know our toilets are all out back in Soweto, in those l'l sheds," she started out, "Satiddy I was walkin' past ours to get to the watah spigot out the-ah when I hear' a funny li'l noise inside the toilet. So I stop' 'n listen. Yassum, it were a funny sound like an animal inside our shed. I thought, 'Thass funny,' so I went inside and there, right on the floah nex' to the toilet was a bundle making them funny sounds." She stopped stirring and glared at me. "Inside that bundle was a baby, a real live baby, only ver', ver' little," she said, shocked.

Her outrage was so powerful that she got up and walked into the breakfast alcove and slammed her broom against the table before she could control herself enough to come back to her tea.

"I didn' know what to do. Mebbe someone who left him were comin' back. He seem still alive, makin' them funny sounds, but I'se mad. Imagine puttin' a little baby out the-ah all alone. It were cold."

"Was it a boy or a girl?" I asked, belatedly realizing that made no difference, but I really didn't know what to say in this situation.

"Yassum. I looked. It were a boy."

"Do you know whose it was?" I asked. "Maybe they could explain what happened," I offered feebly. This was a situation beyond me, and I couldn't offer any explanation or comfort.

"Yas'm. I think I know who it was. She's still a little gull, not marryin' age yet. But I see her goin' to the train, and she lives near me. Always wearin' them big dresses. Guess she was coverin' up. She fooled me," Elizabeth continued.

"An' the baby wasn' black, he were *pink!*" she added, still furious. With that I could understand her fury a little better. I knew that black babies when born are of a very slightly darker skin color than white babies, with facial features that indicate black parentage. It was not unknown for young black women to be taken advantage of by their employers. Of course a somewhat white baby indicated sexual relations, consensual or otherwise. Apparently this baby boy was not wanted by his mother.

"I'se mad, real mad. I went to my neighbor and said, "Whut we gonna do 'bout this?"

"And what did she say?" I asked, totally engrossed.

"She said, 'We gotta get this baby and bring him in, or he gonna die.'" Elizabeth shook her head and went to the teakettle to refresh her tea.

"So we went back there, but the baby was already dead. We unwrapped him. He had a purty blanket 'round him, but he didn' make any more sound. He was quiet 'n dead!"

With this Elizabeth tidied up her tea things noisily and said, "I gotta go clean Miz Wood's flat, Miz Betty. She'll start yellin' if I don't. Thanks for listenin'. I'll let you know what happen." She picked up her cleaning things and left, slamming the door behind her.

HER MOTHER'S HOUSING

Elizabeth brewed her Five Roses tea bag for ten minutes, not five like most people do. She looked at my amber-colored tea and sniffed,

"It's pale. No taste. But lotsa sugah make it nice," she said. Deftly she ladled five spoonfuls into her own dark cup, poured in the milk and noisily stirred it for a few minutes. Finally, content with the fragrance, but brooding over her latest complication in life, she leaned back and sighed,

"It so heavy," she said, shaking her head. "The rents they go up to 17 pounds, not rand, *pounds*." Elizabeth grew up when South Africa was part of the British Commonwealth, so she often thought in pounds, worth about twice as much as the rand.

"Rents go up soon, I dunno when. My mothah, she must pay or they throw her out," she said, emphasizing the point by handing me a letter, warmed from her bosom.

I took it, noting the printed letterhead "Soweto Council." This was official and in English. Knowing Elizabeth's meager education was only to Standard Four (second grade) and in Zulu, not English, I feared there might be a problem she wouldn't understand, but I might.

The letter announced formally that such-and-such house must be emptied unless the rent, now in arrears, was paid by seven days from date. Officials of the Soweto Council would do this. The rent in arrears was R27.55. I noted the date and realized the seven-day grace period was up four days ago. She held up the seven rand that she had so far, and said, "We must make a collection t'night, and my sistah, she'll pay tomorrah."

Since the extra money was considerable, I asked her how she would raise it.

"I dunno. We'll make a collection. But no one she is wuhking but me and my brothah. My brothah he have a wife and family, so he can't pay much. One little gull, she'll give us the seven rand. Ah, we are too many. My son David he not good in the head, not want to sleep at my house, so he sleep in the kitchen at my mothah's. They are 14 who sleep at my mothah's house."

"And your house?"

"We are many. Ten sleep at my house." I pictured Soweto with more than a million inhabitants and its acreage of small, cinderblock, three-room homes with corrugated metal roofs and dirt yards packed tightly together. There was one outside toilet for each, but the nearby water tap served four or five houses. There was no electricity in most of the areas.

"Do you have a bed yet?" I asked her, knowing her late husband's people, Xhosa, came in and took the furniture when he died.

"Yes. The Indian he had an old bed, very cheap, and now I have a bed. I don' have a chair to sit, only the bed now. The childrun? They sleep on the floah. They spread a grass mat, but we don' have enough blankets."

"And when it's cold?"

In mile-high Johannesburg there are 120 days of frost, I remembered from my thesis research.

"We spread the blankets we have over everbuddy; then we spread the laundry, all the clothes ovah everbuddy to keep warm. It cold too much."

Tea was finished, so Elizabeth began washing up. I gave her an extra 12 rand to do the laundry for August, but told her to just work until the 12 rand is used up, in two or three weeks, whatever.

"I wuhk all of August," she said firmly, too proud for handouts.

Next day Elizabeth came in early to tell me, with a big smile on her round, moon-like face, "We make the collection!!

"I take ten rand from you, and my brothah she give ten

rand, and the little gull give seven rand, and my sistah, she go today to pay. Woo-woo!" she shouted happily.

And she cheerily went off to finish cleaning the rest of her assigned flats.

HER SISTER FIGULA

During the previous three days of having tea with Elizabeth, the atmosphere had been quiet, rather ominous. She didn't talk, and she gave abrupt answers to my questions. Something was surely wrong. Finally, on Thursday at teatime she said, "My mothah is ver' sick, and my baby sistah she in jail."

"What happened, Elizabeth?" I asked.

"Figula was jes' dancin' in the street for Guy Fawkes Day and they arrest her. They take her and two othah gulls to jail, John Vorster Square, las' Friday, Sat'day 'n Sunday!"

Guy Fawkes Day was a fun celebration in South Africa and in England, commemorating the attempted coup in 1605 when a group of extremist Catholics tried to blow up the Protestant King James I, and his Parliament. Guy Fawkes, one of the Catholics, was arrested in the cellars of the Houses of Parliament the day before the scheduled attack and betrayed his colleagues under torture. Elizabeth wasn't in the least interested in the historical background of Guy Fawkes Day, but was truly indignant that her little sister was in jail.

"She sleep theah first night. Now she in Johannesburg Prison."

"Why was she arrested?"

"I dunno. Guy Fawkes Day. It's day people dance in th' street. Figula she dance in the street with two othah gulls. Her frien'...y'know the people they dress up to dance in the street, so her frien' bring some uniform of police. She bring uniform from home, her uncle's uniform, and all the gulls want some part of uniform to dress up in. Frien', she pass uniform out to her frien's, and the three gulls dance in the street." Her repetition "dance in the street" sounded as if she had memorized it from the police rulebook.

"It against the law to dress in gov'ment uniform, so police

she hit th' gulls hard. Those Afrikaners, when they hit, they *hit*! Sometimes they hit an' kill."

"Figula, she cry and cry. She not eat for three days in that John Vorster Square. Now they take her to court and tell her R100 for bail. That R100 for bail only. She gotta go ta court again 27th November to find out what happen. Then they take her up there," pointing in the direction of the Hillbrow area.

"To the Johannesburg prison?"

"Yes, she there, and it not nice. Th' old ones they hit th' young'uns inside. Figula can't talk. She cry and cry."

"Did she know that it was against the law to dress in government uniforms?" I asked.

"No, she not know. No one evah tell her. We don' know that. Her frien' bring along her uncle's uniform for them t' dress up in t' dance on Guy Fawkes Day, and all gulls want some parts of th' uniform to dance in. They dance outside the fac-try."

"Where's the factory?"

"I dunno. Someplace in Doornfontein," she replied with a vague wave of her hand toward the railroad area. "But they come and hit them hard, and take them to John Vorster Square and now to prison."

"What will happen now?" I asked.

"We all make collection. The boss of the fac-try he give R50, and Dee's mothah'll pick up money an' take clothes to Figula so she c'n come home."

"I suspect the boss is simply deducting the future pay of Figula," I said.

"*Yebo.* Of course he take it from her pay. But he have the money to help us so we c'n make up the R100. I so wurried. She not eat for three days and now in prison. The old ones so mean to new ones. She nevah in prison befoah. We don' know prison."

Elizabeth looked at the clock, "I'se late. I'se got two extra flats today." She continued, saying, "On train las' Friday, Sophie and the othahs they talk about three gulls in jail foah the dancin.' I not know what they talk about. I get home.

They tell me 'Figula in jail.' I say, 'Whuffoah?' They say she in jail foah dancing in street. I say 'I heard this thing on train, but I not know it Figula.' She so young."

I listened with sympathy. I figured she must be about 32 years old.

Elizabeth, her round face downcast with sadness, was looking out the kitchen window, and I sensed she was close to tears.

I got up and freshened her tea and then handed her the sugar.

NEW HOUSE OFFER

Elizabeth arrived at 8:30 one morning flushed and excited. She had received the electrifying notice of a house to rent in the Chiawala section of Soweto. Elizabeth had been on the West Rand Administration Board's (WRAB) waiting list for a house for 18 years with no apparent action. I had gone with her to WRAB two years before to find out why nothing had happened. Since then, they finally had activated her file and sent it to "New CaNAda" (as Elizabeth pronounced it), her local WRAB Headquarters in Soweto,

"They come to my house las' week," she said, "while I wuz at wurk. Can you phone them this week 'cause I no hear from them again and I'se wurried?"

So I had called. Evidently that helped because a few nights later someone came to her door in Jabulani and told her 'The Office' wanted to see her. She stayed home from work to go to the office yesterday and thus wouldn't get paid for that day. There she waited from early morning until 1 or 2 in the afternoon for someone to call her into the office. Finally, they told her that her name had come up and she would get a four-room house to rent in Soweto. The Chiawala township in Soweto, where the new house was located, was a long way from Jabulani where she currently lived. However, the important thing was that she, a widow, and the many children living with her, would have four rooms with a toilet and a water spigot outside in back all of their own.

"But I no can get that new house unless I pay R100 on Monday, 'an if I do, then they give me a numbah an' a key an' deposit," she said happily. Reality soon set in, however, and she said soberly, "But I can't stay home from wurk again. I'll go to office an' pay money, then get the numbah and then come to wurk. My sistah or somebody go to see house. I need to make th' pay. Miz Wood, she funny, she say, 'Elizabeth tell the office they must call you on Sunday, not on a wurk day.' We laugh," she continued wryly.

Since Elizabeth still owed us money for a bucket of soap and a new pair of overalls, plus some furniture we had sold her last year, I hesitated briefly before offering to lend her the R100. But then, of course, we did give it to her. We agreed to a three-month loan to be paid back by washing our clothes. She had tried to repay a number of loans we had given to her before. Her staunch pride wouldn't let her simply take a gift of money from us.

Inflation was making the newspaper headlines. I wondered how these cleaning women could live on the R119 per month they got paid now by the management that handled the flat. She really had tried to repay the loans we'd given to her, but it would take a while. Besides her R119 monthly salary, Elizabeth got R22.50 a month that we gave her for the wash, and R7 from our nearby neighbor Carol for morning dishes and some wash. Elizabeth's train fare had been raised to R8.50 a month, and coal was now R14, candles R2 (there was no electricity in most of Soweto) and a sack of mealie meal R20 per month, plus her monthly R30.80 rent, school uniforms and exercises, as Elizabeth called the books and notebooks. She *really* was living on the edge.

The house that she currently lived in had belonged to her deceased uncle, but since she was taking care of his four children (as well as her own that didn't stay at her mother's), she used one small room for her own. Elizabeth and all of the children had to cook and eat in the kitchen, and the children slept in the living room or wherever there was space. The prospect of having her own four-room house, with two bedrooms, a living room, and a kitchen was a heady thought indeed.

While we were making the bed together, I noticed that Elizabeth had been having a few nips of wine. She smelled strongly of burgundy. That must be what made her so happy and garrulous today. No wonder. I'd celebrate, too.

AGNES AT HER FACTORY

"What's the matter, Elizabeth?" I asked, noticing her worried frown as she made tea, set out cups, a small pitcher of milk and the sugar bowl.

"Nuthin'" she replied.

I wondered if it had to do with the forms that she and her family had to turn in for her new house. It had been over a week ago that she told me about the possibility of getting a house of her own in Soweto, but there were forms from the WRAB that she had to fill out first.

WRAB had forgotten to give her the forms the day Elizabeth took off work to get them in Soweto. So she had to take another day off to finally get the forms. Both days the management here at Bridgeport had docked her pay. Now Elizabeth had the forms. Mrs. Wood was supposed to fill in one set, and Elizabeth's daughters Agnes and Gertrude the others.

Mrs. Wood had first said that she had misplaced them and told Elizabeth that she would have to go back for more forms. Elizabeth was now trying to figure out what to do, since losing another day's pay would be disastrous considering how carefully Elizabeth allotted her salary for each of her expense items.

Elizabeth said to me, "No, I can't take off any more work. Miz Wood still shout because of those las' two days.

While Elizabeth was cleaning my flat, Mrs. Wood called and said she had found the forms.

We both sighed with relief.

"But now you must go back to WRAB with those forms," I said to Elizabeth, "and secure that house they offered you, or you might lose it."

Elizabeth said, "I talk straight with you, Miz Betty. I not

go today because that gull she forgot th' forms. I wait all day Sunday and she not come with th' forms."

I wondered what girl she meant. After some discussion, it turned out that she was talking about her daughter Agnes, who worked someplace in Doornfontein, a suburb close by, and she had forgotten the forms.

The problem was that Agnes and another daughter, Gertrude, had to get their employers to fill out the forms, showing where they work and their pay. Then the papers had to be stamped, signed and notarized before Elizabeth turned them in to WRAB.

"Where does Agnes work?" I asked, trying to be helpful.

"Le's see," Elizabeth said as she brought out a crumpled bit of paper with a telephone number on it.

"This is wheah she wurk," Elizabeth said, showing me the note.

"Why don't you telephone Agnes and remind her to bring you the forms?" I suggested.

"She can't talk telephone 'cept durin' her lunch half hour," Elizabeth said, "an' then if they can't find Agnes, it won' help."

Then she said, "If you call, Miz Betty, they won't be so cross, 'n you c'n give th' message to her boss."

I took the crumpled paper with the telephone number on it. But when I tried to dial it, I discovered it was an incorrect number.

So I asked her, "What's the name of the company?"

Elizabeth tried hard to think of it, frowning worriedly, but clearly she didn't know.

"Shall we take a note to Agnes to remind her?" I asked, but then stopped. "Can she read?" I asked, realizing many blacks could not.

"Yassum," Elizabeth said proudly. "All my childern can."

Elizabeth could barely write her name, some numbers and a few numbers better than others as the telephone problem showed, and she could read better in Zulu than English.

However, I realized my suggestion to write a note to

Agnes would bring more problems because where would Agnes take the note after she signed it? It seemed that Agnes wasn't living where Elizabeth is living.

"Yassum, Agnes could bring th' forms heah," said Elizabeth, but then I realized we were going out to dinner tonight.

"She could leave the forms in my mailbox," I said.

Suddenly the precariousness of the whole operation and those precious forms made me say, "Elizabeth, I'll take you to the factory, if you can find it, and we'll see Agnes personally and get the forms signed."

Elizabeth had to wait for her lunch half hour before we could go, but promptly at 11:58 she returned for our excursion. We started the drive to Doornfontein. Unfortunately the way Elizabeth directed me was the "walkin' way," so we had to maneuver one-way streets and dead-ends. Then, after a few more problems we discovered ourselves on the other side of the railroad tracks from the factory. We parked the car to walk. Luckily, there were metal steps over the tracks. I felt very white and conspicuous, walking past the many black people to the other side of the tracks.

There were butcher shops, cafes, and black people everywhere in the area, but we finally found the grubby entrance to the factory building where Agnes worked, next to the butcher shop. We walked up the filthy steps to the first floor, trying to ignore the smell, and came to a metal door. I opened the door, with Elizabeth shrinking back behind me, and saw a white receptionist.

"I'm looking for Agnes," I said.

"But there's no Agnes here," she woman replied. "I'm sorry."

Elizabeth looked puzzled, then said, "Next floah up?" so we tiredly climbed up to the next floor.

This metal door said, "NO ADMITTANCE," so I rang the bell. A white woman opened the chained door a crack, and I cheerily asked, "Is Agnes here?"

Evidently Agnes was there because the woman smiled,

unchained the door and invited us in.

The name of the factory was Moulin Rouge. It made ballet clothes and sports outfits. The factory was heaped with bolts of cloth. All around were humming sewing machines run by black women, all dressed in smart, striped overalls. The head woman called Agnes, who came to see who was calling for her. She looked surprised. Elizabeth asked her for the forms that Agnes had totally forgotten. She wasn't even embarrassed that we had had to come to her factory for them. Fortunately, she had them in her bag and gave them to Elizabeth.

The white woman warmly told Elizabeth how much they liked Agnes and how well she worked, then asked kindly,

"Is Agnes, perhaps, your sister?" which made both Elizabeth and me smile since Agnes was her daughter.

Then the woman invited her German-speaking husband over to meet us as well. Several of the girls waved to Elizabeth and greeted her. The white woman then filled out Agnes' form and stamped it, explaining to me that her weekly wage of R35 wasn't all that Agnes got. She also received other little allowances, but confided, "I think it best not to write them on the form."

Elizabeth was still upset over having had to come here, and parted with a few pungent words to Agnes before we left.

She also reminded Agnes to get in touch with Gertrude during her lunch half hour to sign her papers, since Gertrude worked not too far away. After that she had to get them back to Elizabeth.

"Agnes could give them back to Elizabeth at our flat," I started to say, but remembered that we were going out to dinner, so that wouldn't work.

"You can leave them in our mailbox," I concluded.

We left the factory, but on our final descent down those metal steps to our car on the other side of the tracks, four well-dressed black men eyed us closely. As we got into the car one of the men said loudly to Elizabeth, "*UmBantu umHlope.*" Elizabeth replied emphatically, "*Yebo!*"

I could understand enough Zulu to realize he was referring to me in some way, so I asked Elizabeth what he said.

"He say I got *you* to take care o' me so he can't catch me, an' he laugh," she replied in an irritated fashion.

"What was he talking about?" I asked.

She pointed to a large blue van with wire walls nearby that was completely filled with black women. Elizabeth explained that these were women the men had caught without their passbooks, and they were being taken to prison. They would stay there until they were called for their trial. At the trial they would be fined R60 each, and if they had it they'd get out, free again.

"The man say he can't catch me 'cause you here t' take care o' me. I *lucky*, then he laugh again."

Elizabeth pointed to her ample left bosom and confided, "I always carry m' passbook heah when I go out. They *always* ask. Yestiddy at lunch they stopped me fur m' pass. I show it to 'em an' they lemme go."

I had taken just two hours out of my day, but those two hours opened my eyes even more to what life was like when you're black in Johannesburg.

CHEEKY WINDOW CLEANER

At long last another window boy. They came and went with speedy regularity. Even with pay of R180 per month, including a place to sleep and cook in the building, and no coal costs, train fare, candles, water and rent (as Elizabeth bitterly pointed out), they found it difficult to live on that salary. She couldn't be blamed for being somewhat bitter. She earned far less and had to pay her own rent. Elizabeth explained the boys found the pay too low because they had several wives and many children, and they couldn't send much money home out of that.

Several of the men working here in the flat had second jobs. For example, I knew the nice night watchman, who was Zulu, quietly worked days at the Holiday Inn at the airport. He was a chef there making R400 per month. He was doing it because he hoped to be transferred to the Uhlungu Holiday Inn near Zululand after three years. He said nothing here about his other work, but privately told us that after six months, he would leave his Bridgeport job. I wondered how secure our car was in the garage. He must have had to sleep *some* time, but basically we didn't blame him and cooperated in keeping quiet.

Peter, the furnace boy who kept the furnace going and stoked the coal for hot water, worked as night watchman in a nearby building after his hours here, starting there about 7 p.m. Peter had two wives in Venda land and surely many children.

The new window boy here in Bridgeport was called David. He was a Xhosa from the Transkei. Bright, (almost too cleverly) articulate, and I was told, a good worker. When I had complained earlier to the manager, Mrs. Wood, that my windows hadn't been cleaned for four months, she explained that the window boys came and went before they made it up to the seventh floor. So the day when Elizabeth informed me there was a new window boy, I hastily called Mrs. Wood to get my windows done before he could leave.

Shortly after, there was a loud knock at the door. When I opened, it I saw a small, wiry-looking black worker standing there with a ladder, bucket and squeegee.

"I'ze David!" he said, introducing himself. "I'ze here to clean th' windows. Miz Wood said you didn't have your windows cleaned since you bin here."

That was a slight exaggeration, but I didn't want to quibble.

"That's right," I said. "The windows facing the street are particularly sooty with coal dust, and having them clean will certainly let more light in."

He came in and casually looked around our flat, then pulled his short ladder over to the group of windows behind our small entertaining area.

Our social seating area was furnished with a small bamboo settee and had cabinets on each side with two bamboo chairs facing it. Most of our living room was occupied with work areas for Jack and me. There were two large office desks, two filing cabinets and a bookcase for each of us on opposite sides of the room. Jack had his lectures to prepare each day, and my side was a working area for my Ph.D. research and writing.

Noting that David's window cleaning ladder was very short, I told him, "You can stand on one of the cabinets if you use newspapers." His shoes were dirty and looked like he had worn them climbing up the outside wall of the building.

"You should wear tennis shoes for safety," I added, "rather than such heavy ones."

He ignored my remark, but slowly walked around our flat, pausing thoughtfully while studying the various Ndebele beaded items I had hung on the wall. Displayed there were a variety of African art pieces such as an elaborately beaded goatskin cape that an Ndebele respondent had made for her gala dress. It still had the fur on it, and she had woven an intricate, lacey beaded border around the edges. There was also an elegant Ndebele goatskin-wedding apron that had white beads carefully sewn onto every inch of its surface.

Months later, after my fieldwork was over, I had gone back into the field to purchase these notable items from different artists. I had felt, somehow, that it was unethical to buy anything from my respondents while actually doing fieldwork. It might influence their answers in some way. However, after interviewing them for my questionnaire, I had always repaid them for their time by giving them packages of dried fruit, cans of tuna or bars of soap.

As David started cleaning the windows, he suddenly asked, "Madam have a shop?" after having noted all the Ndebele beadwork on the walls.

"No, just writing a book on beadwork," I replied, improvising an answer. How do you explain African art fieldwork for a dissertation?

"What'd you pay f'r that?" he asked, pointing to one of the Ndebele beaded skin aprons.

"Two hundred rand," I said truthfully, and he whistled.

"Where'd you buy it?" he asked.

Rather than trying to explain fieldwork and remembering that Race Relation's Operation Hunger sold Ndebele beadwork, I launched into an explanation of the organization and their support of Operation Hunger, a nonprofit organization that paid the Ndebele women artists directly.

He listened, skeptically, I felt. He then proceeded to ask the price of almost everything visible. Perhaps he was planning on doing some fieldwork of his own?

"C'n I have some music?" he asked.

I reluctantly agreed because while the loud heavy beat of Zulu music might be a great background for physical labor, it certainly wasn't for thesis writing.

On the other hand I might learn something about the music…

David walked over to my fieldwork tape recorder to turn

on the radio, but then realized it was no radio. When I noted his mistake, I handed him my small kitchen radio. He carefully tuned it and we then had the exclamations, shouts and shrieks of a Zulu commercial along with the lovely lullaby sounds of the language. Between commercials the Zulu music's heavy beat came through fine, and David was happy.

When Elizabeth arrived shortly afterward, she raised her eyebrows at the cacophony, but said nothing. David could have cleaned the windows in two hours—others did, I'm sure—but he was so entranced with the music, he slowly cleaned the windows for three and one half hours, carrying the radio everywhere. When he finally folded up his ladder and lovingly polished my little portable radio before handing it back, he asked, "Madam can give David some takkies?"

"Takkies" were tennis shoes. He had noted three pairs that had been put out ready for the "shoe-goo" repair patches. I had to explain, "I'm sorry, but Elizabeth gets all of our old clothes and shoes."

He let it go at that.

Elizabeth had earlier warned me that "David likes his drink."

Evidently on his first day working he had inquired about the nearest bottle store from other workers in the building and then spent the weekend very drunk.

Then, when she first heard him speak, she realized he spoke Xhosa, a language with many more clicks in his speech than Zulu, and her eyes widened. With eyebrows raised and real concern on her face, she whispered hoarsely to me, "Xhosa? *Be careful of your books!*"

Elizabeth had been married to a Xhosa, and when he died, his family descended upon her house and promptly took everything movable, even their bed.

Among the blacks, there were behavior and job stereotypes. For example, in South Africa, the Shangaan from Mozambique cleared the rubbish bins and did the street cleaning, wearing their colorful hand-embroidered coveralls that they had learned to make while recuperating from mine injuries. Perhaps that was why the Shangaan were the rubbish people here.

Also in South Africa, the Zulu were always the policemen, while the Sotho worked in the mines. The Xhosa were considered the educated ones. That stereotype could have had its roots in the fact that the Loveday Mission in the Transkei area was the first place that published books in the vernacular. Thus, many of the Xhosa got an education and could read. At any rate, Elizabeth would say, "The Xhosa are the educated ones, the smaht ones." Thus, when she surveyed our small flat packed with books, and knowing how much we loved them, she wanted us to be extra careful of thievery on the part of this Xhosa, David. Drinking aside, he was a Xhosa, and therefore our books were at risk.

I realized four days later that Elizabeth had been right. David was fired for stealing R200 out of one of the flats. A tenant had tucked the rent money into a dresser drawer and now…the manager of the Bridgeport block of flats was again looking for a window boy.

SECTION III.

Ndebele women and children in front of painted house © Elizabeth Schneider

STRIKE PARADE

I was home sorting slides of decorated mud huts taken on my final field trip for my thesis. Outside I heard the slow heavy thump of drums vibrating up Jorissen Street. I raced upstairs to the outside terrace on the 11th floor and saw several puzzled cleaning women looking down on the procession of university students slowly marching past, protesting apartheid on the anniversary of the student killings in Soweto on June 16, 1976. The mood was somber, in sharp contrast to the joyous parade of Wits students many years before.

One of the cleaners, bewildered by the students' solemn parade, asked, "Why the signs?"

A few women laboriously translated the English words: "Enough of Apartheid!" and "No work today!" There were complaints and mutterings. Early in the morning in Soweto, they had dodged Black Power vigilantes who insisted the women not go to work today to show the government their unanimous protest against apartheid. But Elizabeth and her friends needed to earn money. If they didn't show up, especially on June 16, their white employers wouldn't pay them.

Distressed, Elizabeth turned to me and asked, "Why those students not want us to go to wuhk? Why they want us to not earn money? Don't they *ca'ah*?"

Care? I thought. *How could these women not understand that the students were risking their lives by protesting almost 40 years of apartheid? They were marching and urging workers to stay home and not come to work in order to support all blacks. It was one of the few ways the students could show the government the urgent need for change.*

I responded with, "But they *are* supporting you."

"What you mean?" she asked.

I realized that the enormity of the paradox was too

complicated to explain, given our language barriers. The students were protesting the apartheid system, but the cleaning women who were struggling just to feed their families didn't understand the purpose of the students' protest. They needed to work each day to be paid; moreover, they had good reason to fear they might be killed trying to get home.

I also was worried for their safety getting home once the protest parade ended.

"We mus' go home early befoah they come outta chuch. If we stay 'til 4 o'clock like Miz Wood say, they kill us. They burn our house, they hit us. The police, they theah in CaNAda railroad station (a township in Soweto, one or two train stops before Elizabeth's Jabulani station), but they not theah in Jabulani." Without protection and uncertain how the police would behave in Jabulani, Elizabeth was truly fearful.

"Today we told not to come to wuhk. The train not full. The peepul who stay home, they tell us, 'You go to wuhk, then when you come home, *we fix you*!'

"This mornin' no one t' help us, no taxi, no bus. They hit some people with stones. No one come so we walk. The people that not wuhk, the othahs, they say, 'You not go to wuhk. Why you go to wuhk?' Miz Wood not care if we get killed," Elizabeth shrugged. "She get anothah gull."

"If we come heah, we have big problem when we go home. A man there this mornin' tell Joyce, '*Uyaphi?*'" which was Zulu for "where you going?"

"She say, 'To take my children. I not wuhk today.'"

"Miz Wood alwas say, 'If you not come to work, we not pay you.' Why she not let us go home early? We have to give our key at 1 o'clock when we go to lunch, and then we go back to Miz Wood to get key in afternoon. Ever'buddy else, in other flat buildings with other managers, she go home at 11 o'clock, I think. Big signs tell us not to go to wuhk today. We mus' get home uhly before they finish prayin' at chuch."

"The train police, they clevah. They stay in th' station. Outside, where the peepul at," she said, indicating the overhead bridge at each station, "they not go theah. The stones come down on the train and on us. So now the train go only to CaNAda. We gotta get out an' walk all th' way to Jabulani. We scared all th' way home."

Finally we went back downstairs. Elizabeth and I took our tea break while listening to the 11 o'clock news on South African Broadcasting Company (SABC). In clipped British tones the journalists announced, "All quiet on the Witwatersrand and Durban and Pietermaritzburg, but in the Cape, only 10 percent of garment workers came to work. Coloureds are boycotting work. Blacks as well." I knew that in the Cape there were few blacks. Most non-whites were coloured.

"Turn on Zulu station," said Elizabeth. We listened to the lyrical, vowel-heavy sounds of Zulu, but at a rising pitch, heavy with tension. It sounded nothing like the Zulu lullaby songs we learned in my varsity's Zulu class the previous week. I couldn't understand any of the words, but I did understand the tension.

Elizabeth listened intently. "They say nuthin' 'bout th' strike, but say they'll report it at 1 o'clock."

Joyce, Elizabeth's close friend, came to the door and said, "Thelma just came to wuhk. She shakin' like this," she said as she graphically displayed hands fluttering. "She say it quiet in township, but some man tell her, 'Bettah not go to work.' She can hardly talk she so scared."

Elizabeth returned and sat down, refreshing her tea and adding five spoonfuls of sugar before the milk, indicating a . real crisis.

"Joyce, she so scared. Too bad. She sick. She got high blood, and now she so scared, she be sick again. I go now to see Miz Wood. If she say we can go now, we go home. We clean passages now and go. But if she say no, you see me heah this aftanoon at 2 o'clock cleanin' passages."

Elizabeth paused, then resumed, "At Clifton Heights," the block of flats across the street, "the gulls all gone at 11 o'clock. They let them go. But Miz Wood, *nevah*! The train people" – guards and engineers – "stay away from trouble., They tired of powah." Everyone knew the Zulu word used in the protests was *Amandla*' with fist raised. "Train peepul they stop the train in CaNAda. The Putco," the bus company for blacks, "they put their buses away. No taxis. They tired of all the breakin' things.

"Yestiddy we go home uhly. We walk with no bags or nothin'. And when people say, 'Wheah you come from?' we say we at chuch, the one ovah theah. We don't say we at wuhk. They kill us. We just walk."

"Did you walk alone or with friends together?"

"We walk alone. We all live ovah theah. No one help when this happen. You by yourself. No one say anythin'. They scared. We just walk along." She demonstrated the trudge of someone walking a long distance. "If we walk from CaNAda, it long walk. Our feet, we think we can't come to wuhk tomorra. When we walk today, we no carry bags. They think we no come from Jo-burg. Bettah that way."

"The new gull Olga, upstairs on ninth, she come to wuhk, but she say her children cry and say, 'Why you go to wuhk? They kill you and then we have no mothah.' Her husban', she stay home today. She not wuhk, but Olga come..."

Suddenly we heard much knocking at the door. Anxious conversations took place between the cleaning women, all about work. They wondered when they could go home. Elizabeth explained they were comparing reports of what they had heard from each worker here.

Their rapid speech was too much for my two years of Zulu classes, but you didn't need to know Zulu to feel their fear.

THE ACADEMIC AND THE RADIO

By the mid-1980s it had become unsafe to walk the six blocks to the university, in contrast to our arrival in South Africa in 1975. One day I prepared for my fortnightly drive to another neighborhood for groceries, because the local, dismal OK Bazaar was tolerable only for emergencies. Elizabeth was doing wash in our bathtub, and Jack was preparing his lectures on the balcony.

"Jack, this radio should be fixed soon; the reception is so bad."

"Which radio?"

This one," and I held up our tiny, silver-colored shortwave radio. I finished breakfast and went out for the groceries. On returning three hours later, Jack greeted me by announcing, "The big black radio has come back."

"Come *back*?" I asked, puzzled.

"Yes," he replied cheerfully. "A white man came up here with George, the watchman, while you were gone. Elizabeth was busy, and the man was carrying our big, black radio-cassette player. I asked him how much, and when he didn't say anything, I assumed you had taken it to the shop, giving a price limit on repairs, and so the store sent it back un-repaired. Therefore, I gave the man 50 cents."

"I did not take the big radio in for repairs." He looked startled. We rushed into the bedroom to see if what had been returned really was our radio. It was indeed. We looked at each other trying to fathom what had happened.

"Were you here all the time?" I asked.

"Yes, except five minutes when I walked around the block, but Elizabeth was here all the time."

"Where were you sitting?"

"On the balcony next to our bedroom, working on

lectures and having my tea," Jack said.

He had been sitting six feet away from the big, black radio-cassette by our bed.

"And Elizabeth?" I asked.

"In the bathroom washing clothes, except when she hung them on the balcony."

We looked at each other, totally puzzled.

"Wait!" Jack said, and hurried down to the foyer to ask George, the current watchman in our building.

"*Yebo* boss, I see this white man come in without a radio, and he come out with a radio, so I ask him -- 'cause I think somethin' funny – 'Where you get radio?' He say, 'I take it for repairs and bring it back, but the people not home.'

"I say to him, 'Take me to flat where you get radio,' and we go up to flat 605. No one there, so I say 705?' and he say 'Yeah, flowers or somethin' in front,' and I bring him to the boss." He nodded toward Jack.

"The boss he smile and give the man 50 cents, so I think it must be OK. In the lift the man show me 50 cents and say, 'See, he gave me money,' so I think it must be all right."

With that information, we checked and discovered our flat door was unlocked. Even with Elizabeth in the bathroom washing and Jack probably on the balcony writing, the man had walked in, calmly disconnected the radio, aerial, earphones and walked out carrying the big, black radio-cassettte player without anyone seeing or hearing him.

"So the watchman George is our hero," I said.

After that experience, we firmly locked the door even when inside. But viewing the size of our small flat, with bedroom and balcony, minute living-room and kitchen alcove, the image of a third person inside, between Jack and Elizabeth (about 15 feet apart) calmly disconnecting and stealing a big radio-cassette player, was astounding.

"He was cheeky, he was," was Elizabeth's summary.

At the bar that night, I'll bet the burglar amazed his cronies with that tale of attempted burglary: not getting caught, and then being paid 50 cents for trying.

WHERE'S ELIZABETH?

"What's been going on? What's that stain on the floor? And those slivers of glass?" Jack asked. We had just returned to our flat in South Africa in 1987 from one of our many research trips to Brazil. Jack had noticed an odd mark on the floor,

I looked to see what he was pointing at, with shock. "It looks like bloodstains, doesn't it? Someone tried to sweep up those glass splinters but didn't get them all. Whatever happened here?" We had thought we were safe in our small apartment in South Africa, but apparently blood had moved out of the streets and into our apartment.

The violence, euphemistically called "unrest" by the government, was pervasive in the Johannesburg area. Every day we saw in both the Afrikaans and English newspapers disturbing reports about strikes, protests, and car-jacking murders. In the liberal English press we read about the torture and killing of political prisoners by the government. Whenever we took a plane, we'd see the crowds of journalists and other international media coming in with their aluminum trunks of film and camera gear to report and photograph the South African violence for the outside world. We felt like observers on the edge of history, but unfortunately this history was bloody and violent.

"Four Car-Jackings in Downtown Joburg," proclaimed one newspaper.

"Traffic Halted in Braamfontein for Weapons Search," announced another.

That last event happened to be something I'd been involved in. Soldiers had stopped all traffic on Jorisson Street, one of the main arteries from the university into downtown. They were scrutinizing drivers and opening the boots (trunks to Americans) of each car to see if anyone was carrying guns or bombs.

That was the situation in South Africa when Jack was invited in the late 1980s to be a Visiting Professor at the University of Campinas in Sao Paulo, Brazil. There, I continued working on the literature research part of my dissertation. Sometimes we would be in Brazil for several months at a time, but we always kept our flat in Johannesburg, which was home.

It had been comforting when we left Johannesburg to lock up our flat and to experience the secure feeling people have who live in flats and travel. You simply double-locked the door and relaxed, knowing there was a day and night watchman and secure lifts. It was much safer than leaving a house empty, we thought, because our flat was on the seventh floor, and there was no outside access to the lift except through the lobby, past the watchman. Nor was there an accessible window facing the corridor on the seventh floor. Some flats had locked, protective iron doors in front of their main door, but not ours.

True, there was an open terrace on the 11th floor where residents and staff would sometimes gather to watch what was happening on the street far below or to observe the breathtaking sunsets. I can remember the irony of watching a magnificent lavender, pink and yellow sunset above while hearing gunshots by the police and ambulance sirens rushing past below.

We had felt secure in our flat. The 11th floor terrace had a spiked iron fence atop the brick wall. How could anyone rappel down a wall with few handholds from the 11th floor to the seventh? How could a person then navigate across the sheer vertical wall of three flats to get to ours on the north side? It seemed impossible, but evidently someone did do this, and then smashed our living room window to crawl inside. I wonder if the thief had any idea that the foreigners' only treasures were our books, file cabinets and one small boom box with a tape player.

Apparently, according to our next-door neighbor who told us about it later, "The thief was cut so badly by the broken window glass that he got no farther. Josiah, the watchman, had heard the shattering glass, and promptly called the manager, Mrs. Wood."

Evidently when she unlocked our door, she found the thief bleeding badly on our living room floor. The police came and took him away.

This event had happened about a month before we returned from Brazil. No one had notified us. At Mrs. Wood's insistence, the working staff had done their best to clean up all the evidence. They replaced the window, swept the floor repeatedly, but we could still see something unusual had happened. Mrs. Wood downplayed the event, hoping we would not move out.

I was anxious to hear Elizabeth's trustworthy version of the tragic event, but apparently she had been ill and was not coming to work very often, if at all.

I knew it was dangerous for Elizabeth or for any of the blacks to take the train in from Soweto during South Africa's state of emergency. But many did ride in because they needed their wages to support an extended family. I hoped someone from Soweto could give me information about where Elizabeth was, or her family, but no one seemed to know.

There was simply no way I could reach Elizabeth. By now whites were not allowed into Soweto with its extreme violence and danger. She had no phone. Her good friend Joyce no longer worked at our building, and the new flat cleaners didn't know Elizabeth and so couldn't tell me what had happened to her. Only Elizabeth could be trusted to tell us the real story of what had happened. Certainly not the flat manager. But Elizabeth was missing. I worried that she might have been a victim of the violence as well.

I was terribly frustrated thinking Elizabeth might be ill with her chronic heart problem or possibly killed in Soweto, or perhaps even in our apartment.

I was desolate and deeply upset.

ESCALATING VIOLENCE

Several times during the 1980s the South Africa government officially declared a State of Emergency. Our State Department warned Americans not to travel to South Africa because of the serious danger, and travelers from other countries were notified as well. In general, because of the widespread riots during that decade, it was safer for us to make ourselves as inconspicuous as possible to all armed authorities.

We were in the midst of a revolution, and we were scared. I had to finish my thesis, and Jack had to finish his teaching contract with the university, which had another year to go.

A white male social worker who had been working in Soweto for years had recently been murdered there. He was a deeply respected social worker. Many black people as well as whites were furious about it. The whole country was risky and explosive, and Johannesburg was the worst because of its high concentration of blacks.

As in many revolutions, the good people trying to improve a situation are often the first ones eliminated one way or another, no matter what their skin color. In their haste, the black and white South African police and army, trying to gain control of a violent situation, were just as likely to eliminate protesters by their skin color, which is plainly visible and quicker to discern, than by people's politics. Skin color, for police and army personnel in a hurry, clarified the battlefield by removing the ambiguous gray area between the good guys and bad guys who came in both skin colors.

Or new violence might erupt because of the lingering antagonisms of the 1900 Boer War between white Afrikaners and Brits. The blacks and whites in the police or army would attack both white and black political liberals, or use their firepower to settle old animosities.

We could no longer walk the six blocks to the university but had to drive our car, making our way through locked iron gates to park safely on campus. Constant warnings on the radio advised us, when stopping at a traffic light, to leave enough space between our car and the one in front of us so we could drive away rapidly if someone tried to smash the car window to carjack the car. Some thieves used a heavy metal arm guard to more quickly crash through the safety glass, pull up the door lock to open the door, pull the driver out and kill him.

When I did try to drive to the university, frequently all the cars were stopped by soldiers walking back and forth, checking each car for guns or bombs in the back seat, on the floor, or in the trunk. It was a tinderbox situation. If someone shouted during these stops, I cowered low in my car because there was no way of knowing what or where the trouble was. I just wanted to get into the locked iron gates enclosing our university campus or return to our building's basement garage safely.

The incredible ferocity that was going on could scarcely be believed. We learned from the papers and television about necklacing, a horrendous fate that happened to a number of blacks that were thought by other blacks to be informers. Several accusers would single out a suspect, handcuff him and then, after seating him on the ground, hang an old tire around his neck. The tire was then filled with gasoline and set alight. As the flames engulfed the victim, you could see him struggle and fall over as the fire roared around his body. There were many unbelievably horrific necklacings.

None of the liberals, no matter what skin color, trusted either the police or the army, and with reason. One of our anthropology lecturers, David Webster, born in Zambia, was a close friend whose office was next to mine. David had always been politically active. He was the one who held tea parties for faculty, students and staff where we brought textbooks that David tried to deliver to the many students and faculty who had been imprisoned for so-called "subversive activities."

For delivering educational materials, the secret Special Forces of the Police Department felt David Webster was an enemy to be eliminated. They targeted his home, and then one of their white agents brutally murdered him on May Day, 1989, a Sunday morning when he emerged to walk his dogs.

"Impossible!" we said when those of us working that weekend in the Anthro Department heard about it. David had promised to read my dissertation the next day.

Horrified, we asked Maggie, his longtime companion, what had happened.

Sobbing, she replied, "He always walked his dogs in the morning, and just as he got their leashes on and out the door for their walk, a white police van sped out of a side street. I heard some shots, and the van skidded around the corner and took off."

She had seen the whole thing.

"I rushed out. He was lying there on the sidewalk. I held his head in my lap. It was all bloody. I told him he had to live. We needed him. He tried to say something but couldn't. He just turned his head and died right there." (Years later, during the Truth and Reconciliation period, the Police Special Forces killer confessed his crime. He was denied amnesty and punished, since David's murder was considered not justified.)

Life became even more frustrating for me because the violence had now extended out into my fieldwork area, and no outsider was permitted to travel there. A further complication was a vicious war between the Sotho and Ndebele chiefdoms in that area of the Transvaal Province. Whereas before the two societies had lived comfortably together despite different languages and customs, a violent change had happened.

Much to their dismay, all the Ndebele were told they were going to be settled into the new Ndebele Homeland the South African government was establishing to separate the Sotho people from the Ndebele. The government plan was to create separate Homelands for the various black groups under an overall white-controlled apartheid government. The security forces removed many Ndebele from their traditional lands, and in exchange, dumped them in their new Homeland, a bleak, arid wasteland with little or no shelter or water. Some Ndebele people were able to retrieve a few of their corrugated iron roof panels from their mud huts, but little else.

The hereditary Ndebele Paramount Chief was battling a politically acquiescent Headman, appointed by the South African government, for position and power. The surrounding Sotho people either sided with or battled with both groups. But most people in the area, no matter what nationality, fought against the South African government because they did not want this enormous and devastating exchange of cropland for wasteland.

For me the situation was disastrous. To obtain a government permit to follow up my early interviews was impossible. And I had a dissertation deadline. Gloomily I settled down to write up my fieldwork and collect everything together for the dissertation. It had taken me almost ten years, and it was high time to finish.

To add to my gloom, I had not been able to gather any information about Elizabeth, such as whether her health had improved or whether her lodger-friend Jack (who always said "ta ta" when leaving) was still with her. What had happened to her? Was she safe? She would have commiserated with me about the abrupt end to my fieldwork. She might have been able to add some information from her daughter Agnes who had married an Ndebele and was now living in the Ndebele Homeland. Most importantly, she could reassure me that she was in good spirits, good health, and her large family intact.

CHICKEN RUN

"We've got to pack our things for the shipping container," Jack said, as our many years in South Africa drew to a close. He was right. The bloodshed and ferocity had increased, and it wasn't safe to remain in Johannesburg. We were back there again, having just returned from the last of our many stays at the University of Campinas in Brazil, and Jack's dictionary research there was now finished. By 1989 it was time to pack for California. We knew Jack's work would require us to return later for short stays in rented accommodations.

Yes, it was time to go home. No more showing the contents of my purse whenever I went to the supermarket, cinema or other public place. No more noting at the airport how many foreign journalists were coming in with their aluminum suitcases full of camera equipment to show the world the brutality and carnage that was going on in South Africa.

I started packing up our books and looked around at the other things we had acquired over the years. Oh yes, the dining room table that Jack had made. That table would go with us for sure.

Jack had worked hard on the table, which became our favorite piece of furniture. It was where we often entertained friends at dinner. He had found a rough Africa Cable spool discarded in the Senate House basement by the workmen after the spool was emptied. Jack had laboriously rolled the heavy spool home and, with Josiah and Peter's help, got it onto our balcony. There, Jack sanded it, painstakingly plugged up all the nail holes and varnished it. On the maroon underside he left the large white letters identifying the Africa Cable company.

As I advertised our bed and other furniture for sale, I was

amused to see how many other people wanted that table. We would never part with it. It was a tangible reminder of Jack's handiwork, which had never been outstanding before. During my many weeks out in the field doing research, he had labored over that large, cable spool. Somehow, we felt it represented much of our life in South Africa. We both loved it.

I happily packed up the useful little bench that Elizabeth had given to me one Christmas. "For when you to sit outside your house each day in the sun," she had said, "like we do!" It still has a place of honor next to my bed.

Also the many African art pieces I had purchased, after I had finished my fieldwork, of course.

One thing gnawed at me while I was packing up flat 701. I had finally finished my thesis and handed it in. My orals were now completed and the internal examiners had passed everything, but the department had not yet heard from the two external examiners. Much to my dismay, I found that I would not be able to take part in the graduation ceremony. It was a profound disappointment. I had already signed up for the graduation banquet, rented my handsome red Ph.D. robe and its accompanying black velvet tam o'shanter, which resembled a pizza draped over one's head. In my fantasies I had pictured myself in graduation gear, holding my graduation scroll, standing next to one of the enormous pillars that graced the front of Senate House. That picture would be tangible evidence I could repeatedly look at, knowing that I had finally finished school after 45 challenging years, but it was not to be.

We reluctantly told our South African friends we were going and took part in the many farewell parties for us, just as we had earlier attended farewell parties for the many friends that had already departed. We found ourselves joining the "chicken run," as the locals called the exodus. While bidding them adieu, I felt sad at what had happened to the post-college age children of our many friends. Feeling there was no future for them in South Africa, they had left the continent with their parent's blessing. It was heart wrenching. The country sorely needed them.

"We raise them to export," one mother had said to me, mournfully. "There is no future for them here."

"Why don't you go with them?" I naively asked several friends.

"Our lives are here. The small amount of rand currency that the government would permit us to take out wouldn't last three months on the outside," they explained.

Both Jack and I, as permanent foreign residents, were fully aware of that problem. Whenever we had made vacation plans to go to Europe or to the U.S., we had to comply with the law stamped in our passport limiting us to carrying only R1,000 (the value of which vacillated widely) by making and paying in rands well in advance for flights and hotel reservations from South Africa.

Outside of South Africa, no South African or permanent foreign resident was allowed to have an American credit card, savings account or even an American checkbook that would enable us to have the use of more money outside.

The authorities carefully examined each departing traveler to be sure we had no more money on us, which spawned many local tales. The favorite urban myths were descriptions of how someone had been physically examined before getting on an outbound plane.

"He had much of his valuable stamp collection in his mouth" was one.

"They had about ten oriental rugs that they tried to smuggle out as part of their home furnishings" was another.

There were other detailed descriptions that couldn't be told in polite company.

When we left Johannesburg, we were grateful that our books were academic and had not been blacklisted. I remembered that at the downtown public library there was a box of index cards listing books that were banned in South Africa. Curious, I had looked them over after someone told me the children's story of the horse "Black Beauty" was one of them, but I was never able to verify it.

Loading our boxes into the Bekins Overseas Moving van, double-parked in front of our flat building, was an interesting operation, especially compared to moving in the States. In Johannesburg, four men handled our move: two movers, a security man and one driver. The driver had to stay seated in his van to keep the police from moving him on. The three others proceeded with the intricate dance of the boxes being moved from our flat to the truck. It was a remarkable demonstration of eliminating thievery, being cautious and caring for the safety of our boxes.

I noted one mover stood by the back of the truck's van to receive the numbered and labeled boxes, meanwhile counting them. Two other movers came up the lift to our flat. One picked up the boxes and rode down in the lift, accompanied by the other, a Bekins security man who did not touch the boxes or let anyone else touch them.

In the end, all boxes and Jack's table arrived safely in California many, many months later. Their route started in a truck from Johannesburg to the Durban seaport on the Indian Ocean, then by ship westward around the bottom of Africa, crossing the Atlantic to the Pacific Ocean via the Panama Canal, then up the west coast of Central America and the United States to the Port of Oakland, near San Francisco.

The ballet of the Bekins Overseas movers is one of my lasting memories of Johannesburg.

VOTING AT LAST: 1994

April 27, 1994, would be a significant day in South Africa. There was going to be the very first multiracial election held in South Africa in 46 years, so we arranged to be there for a short work visit.

It seemed as if everyone had been waiting for the election. After all, it was the first election in many years in which the vast majority of the population would finally get to vote. The excitement was palpable. From the many people permitted, at last, to have a voice in their government, to those guarding the ballot boxes, and others counting the votes, all the way up to the police and soldiers assigned to keep order – everyone was excited.

The Sowetan (the biggest newspaper for the blacks) had printed articles about it for several weeks before this day. *The Star,* the establishment newspaper, wrote about it. *The Mail/Guardian,* the most liberal newspaper read by the progressive English-speaking whites, discussed it at length. Even the all-Afrikaans newspaper *De Beeld*, had things to say about it.

I heard that the cleaning women in our building had been buzzing about their plans to get up very early that morning and wear their best Sunday clothes while waiting in the lengthy lines to vote.

"This, our day at last!" our new flat cleaner proudly said to me. We had rented a friend's flat for a three month university sojoun (we had continued to move back and forth between Brazil and South Africa for short-term appointments). We were thrilled at the prospect of being able to wind up some unfinished university work *and* be here for the momentous election.

The university administration announced that everyone in

the university, students and faculty alike, was to help as many black workers as possible understand what voting and checking the names on the ballot meant and exactly how to do it.

One cleaning woman at the university described to me how she was going to transport her aged granny in a wheelbarrow so she could also participate in this momentous event.

"She can't walk, but she must vote," she said firmly.

Others talked about how long the actual ballot was, because it would be printed in the 11 different official languages of South Africa. The result was a ballot that extended across the desk, down to the floor and along the floor.

"But I thought the 'X' in front of his name means 'No, not him. Like the bike signs," one man said to me, puzzled, as I was trying to help him understand the ballot. One of the janitors at the university said that he thought the "X" that he was told to use in front of the candidate's name that he wanted, was just the opposite from what he expected. "Didn't the 'X' mean 'No'?" They were accustomed to the circle/slash system used on metal traffic signs for "No Entry" on a one-way street, "No Parking," or "No Bicycles." Because of that, he thought a slash, or an "X," meant he did not want that candidate.

"Should I put an 'X' in front of every name except Mandela's?" the cleaning woman asked.

A student tutor at our university hastily clarified that point for her.

Many volunteers helped those who were illiterate.

Jack and I were excited as well. Even to be in Johannesburg for such a momentous occasion was almost unbelievable.

But the unrest and the raw violence were building up and continuing in town. They worried me deeply. There were more random shootings, car-jackings and muggings. It was not safe on Johannesburg's streets. Although the university was but six blocks away from our flat, by now we always put Jack's wheelchair, the result of a stroke in 1988, into the car, and drove into the university garage, where the huge metal gate clanged and locked shut behind us.

There were many Afrikaners, government people, and probably others who didn't approve of the voting that was about to happen.

My underlying anxiety surfaced the day I heard sirens screaming along the street leading to Johannesburg's Central Library a few blocks down from University Hill. As I was looking out of the Mathematics Department's office window, I could see puffs of gun smoke from shooting below. People were running in many directions and I could hear faint shouting from the uncontrolled shooting going on in the Library Mall, a scarce half-mile away. The noises the library crowd made rose up to University Hill and came through to us in clouds of rising and falling sound. It seemed unreal, as if I were seeing a movie of this startling and unbelievable action.

We should try to get out of this wounded and bleeding country while we still can, I thought. I stumbled to the phone and shakily dialed Lufthansa Airlines. Our flight to Germany, the first leg of our trip back to California, was booked for the following week, but it seemed prudent, indeed urgent, to see if we could get out earlier. When the airline finally answered, I explained hoarsely that while our reservations were for later, my husband and I urgently needed to leave early.

"Would it be possible to exchange our tickets for a flight out as soon as possible?" I asked the clerk, hardly recognizing my own gravelly voice.

ELECTION DAY

"You want to leave before the election?" the Lufthansa clerk asked with disbelief.

She was speaking from her safe location at the Jan Smuts Airport 25 kilometers away from the simmering center of Johannesburg where we lived.

"I doubt we have any seats left on such short notice," she said.

"Would you try?" I asked, trying to keep my shaking voice calm. "We want to exchange next week's business-class tickets."

At the end of my telephone line, I could still hear the ongoing shouting and gunshots at the Library Mall in the distance. There was a long wait while the airline clerk checked for seats.

"Well, ye-s," she said finally. "It looks like you're in luck. Can you come out here three hours early tomorrow? Since your husband can't walk up stairs, he and his chair will have to be hydraulically hoisted up early with the food cabin. I hope you don't mind a long wait."

I would have run the hydraulic lift myself or cheerfully camped overnight in the plane's small food cabin if that was the only way we could get onto that plane. Still, our first barrier was bridged. The next was to get back to our friend's flat and pack. From remote California a few months ago, being here during the election had seemed like such an exciting idea. But exciting in the abstract was quite different from the stark reality.

We quickly made the rounds of our friends, saying something had come up and we had to leave early for California. We felt guilty running out and leaving our South African friends in such an uncertain and dangerous climate. It seemed strangely disloyal for us to turn tail and flee. After all, together we had all weathered the growing turbulence during the '70s and '80s, condemning others who had taken the "chicken run" before us. Why did I feel it imperative for us to leave now? Was it the calm flow of time during those months in California that made me realize how foolhardy it was to push our luck here?

Next morning, I drove us out to the airport, hating our conspicuous red BMW rental car, taking all the back roads to avoid the police blocks and political violence. The police did stop us once, but we said we were on the way to the airport, and they let us pass. Johannesburg seemed to be holding its breath on one hand, yet was full of exuberance and expectations on the other. All I knew was I wanted to leave this place and fly home safely. Opposite to the usual order in my life, I felt I would be much safer in the air than on the ground.

I dropped Jack and our luggage at the corner of the International Building at Jan Smuts Airport. As I unloaded our bags and his wheelchair for him to wait outside for the 30 minutes I needed to return the rental car, I suddenly realized how vulnerable he looked sitting there. I found myself devoutly thinking, *I hope he'll be all right.*

When I got back a short time later, I heaved a great sigh of relief to see all was intact, and he was exactly where I had left him and the bags.

We worked our way to the check-in counter and got our boarding passes. The attendant delivered us to the runway next to the huge hydraulic lift that would deposit us safely aboard, along with large quantities of food and necessities for the passengers and crew on the 12-hour flight to Germany. As we finally settled into our comfortable seats, I felt I could truly breathe for the first time in two days.

The long flight was beautiful, peaceful and quiet. We arrived in Frankfurt utterly exhausted and spent the night in the luxurious airport hotel.

Next morning's newspaper was dropped at our hotel door.

Over breakfast we casually opened it to see how yesterday's election had turned out. Had Mandela been elected?

There, on the front page of the newspaper was an astonishing picture of Jan Smuts Airport. In the picture it was still daylight, and evidently only a short time after we left, there had been an enormous explosion at the International Building.

It was the very same corner where Jack had waited for me with our luggage. Radical Afrikaners had filled a parked Audi with powerful explosives and a timing device set to detonate not long after we took off. A jagged hole marked where an entire corner of the building had been blown up, and there remained a deep crater where the Audi had been parked.

Jack and I sat there, stunned, unable to talk about the extraordinary election and our good fortune.

LETTERS TO BARBARA

Several years after leaving South Africa in 1996, our final visit, I was home clearing the breakfast dishes from what we called our 'Africa table.' Nowadays, upon hearing the story of how Jack had painstakingly transformed this African Cable spool, our dinner guests crouch down to peer at the letters on the underside of the wooden table. It is a strong; memorable South African presence in our permanent home in California.

It was a sunny morning when the phone rang. A woman announced, "This is Barbara Colburn calling long distance from Idaho." It was so unexpected that for a moment I held my breath in disbelief.

"Barbara Colburn! What a remarkable surprise to hear from you. It must be, let's see, 16 years or so since we last saw each other in Johannesburg." Barbara had been my American friend who became intrigued with Elizabeth after reading the observations about her in my journal.

"And you're coming here next weekend to meet with the Resignos?" I asked.

"Yes, next weekend."

"I remember the Resignos well. They introduced us to your family. I do hope we can all get together. There is so much to catch up on."

I couldn't wait to ask the one big question that had been looming in my mind these final few years. Perhaps, just perhaps, Barbara knew what had happened to Elizabeth. That last year Jack and I had been in South Africa had been so turbulent, and I had been trying to finish my thesis in time to graduate before we left. The violence, the shooting and killing had been so intense that there was no way any white person could go into Soweto to go to Elizabeth's house. Even Johannesburg and Durban were aflame.

Despite my questioning everyone in Johannesburg who had known Elizabeth, I had never been able to find out where she was or what had happened to her. It felt like I had a chronic illness that wouldn't heal. I was utterly desolate and frustrated whenever I thought about her: her round cheery face and hearty laugh, her ample build, her dauntless spirit.

As if she read my mind, Barbara asked, "Betty, have you any news about Elizabeth? I've often wondered what happened to her. I think I might have some information, sort of, about her."

"Oh tell me, please, what do you have?" I asked eagerly, but also with foreboding and a somewhat sinking heart. It had been such a long time.

"I can't tell you about it on the phone, but when we get there I'll show you something," was all Barbara would say.

The weekend finally arrived, and our group gathered at a local restaurant. We talked about those memorable, wrenching times in South Africa from the 1970s to the 1990s during the very worst years of apartheid. They had left a mark on all of us who experienced them, even for just a short time, as had Barbara and Walter.

After dinner we invited everyone back to our house for tea and coffee. Soon Barbara came into the kitchen where I was preparing the drinks while the others continued their reminiscences, still vivid.

"Do you remember I started helping Elizabeth with her sweetie business in 1980 with a part of the small legacy my mother left me?"

"Oh, yes, I certainly do."

"Well, when we moved back to the States in 1985, I wasn't sure how to get the money to Elizabeth safely, without someone there in Soweto monitoring it for me to be sure she got it. You were in Brazil when we left. For the first few months, I just sent money orders to her P.O. box in Jabulani from here in the States hoping she would get them, even though I realized that was probably foolhardy."

"Did she send notes thanking you?" I asked.

Barbara replied, "Yes, I think it was someone at her church who would write them for her, and Elizabeth would sign with that wobbly signature and her mixed up letters. Remember how we used to compliment her for finally learning to sign her name?"

"Yes." I remembered vividly when Elizabeth had taken time off from cleaning each day while I taught her to spell and write her name so that the manager would let her open a bank account at Nedbank.

"That was a milestone," said Barbara. "Well, a few months after I came back to the States, I met Angela, a Quaker missionary in Washington who was from South Africa, and I told her the Elizabeth story. Angela said she knew a member of the Friends, Quakers in Soweto, who could look Elizabeth up.

"Angela's Quaker friend in Soweto was named Duduzile Mtshazo, and Duduzile could take a letter and a check to Elizabeth. So I wrote an explanation to Elizabeth and gave the letter and check to Angela to give to Duduzile," who could get it to Elizabeth," Barbara said.

"Wasn't that lucky you found someone from the Friends who might be a contact? Did you ever get a response from anyone?" I asked.

"No. Angela didn't respond, although I wrote to her more than once, and I still kept sending money for about two years to Elizabeth's address, until 1987. When I didn't hear from Elizabeth after sending the last cashier's check, I stopped sending money. I wrote several more letters to Elizabeth, but she didn't answer."

"So that was your news, sort of, about Elizabeth, that you mentioned on the phone?" I asked, but with misgiving. It had been too long.

"No, not all, there's more. Starting a few months after that, I received these letters from Soweto over a period of time," she said, pulling out several letters postmarked Johannesburg, South Africa, that she had bundled into a small packet held together with a rubber band. I took them eagerly and glanced over the messages.

Barbara continued, "A couple of them seemed authentic, but then the others somehow didn't quite make sense to me, knowing all you had told me about Elizabeth and having known her sister Maria and her family," she said.

"That's right. You hired Maria to clean for you, in 1983 was it? She must have talked a lot about Elizabeth, and about their family, too."

"Yes. Well, here's the last letter I got. It's postmarked 1996." Barbara went on, "That signature on this last letter bothered me. It was too good.'

She handed me a beautifully penned letter in a slanted script. I started reading it out loud. "Dear Barb."

"Now that seemed odd," she interrupted. "She never called me 'Barb'; it was always Mrs. Colburn or Barbara." I resumed reading.

> *Please I hav received your letter. I was so very very happy to hear that you still alive with your blessed family and the beautiful photo you hav sent to me. A thousand thanks for your kindness - not only to me but also to God.*
>
> *Oh Barb, myself I am still alive with my familly including Maria's childrens but the only thing most worry is that you have send us some money by Duduzile Mtshazo and whoever get that money from her; and I never see Duduzile for about five to six years -she disappeared forever. But what I heard about people is that she bought a new car and a new house. She don't even come here in Jabulani anymore since 1992, so on. She is now too dangerous to me and to others. Dear Barbara Colburn, Please I plead you – not to send the money by Duduzile anymore.*

> *Dear Barb, I believe you know the old man staying with me here in [number] 1763. – so please send the money by his ID No. 281111535-7-087…his name is Mr. Mandlosi Mondau Johannes.*

Oh!, I thought to myself. *Jack is a common nickname for Johannes. Did her Jack write this letter? I never heard his formal name before. Hmm, Mondau is a Shangaan name from Mozambique, like Jack!"*

Barbara interjected, "And the ID number was carefully repeated. But look what comes next."

> *Please cansel Duduzile; please forget really about her. Now the address of this man is the same – 1763 Jabulani at Koma Street, and you know we stay together. Nothing can be wrong at all. Please try: do try: to believe this new ID number.*

"The writer was repeating it for the third time," Barbara said. "It even included his name again and the Jabulani address of Elizabeth. But read the rest, presumably from Elizabeth."

> *'He is the man I trust him very very much since we are together here from 1980 up to now. Let us trust him. Maria's childs they are also in good condition and they will also be back to schools on January 14, 1997. I can be very very happy if you can send me the money before the end of February. I am so much in difficulties. Dear Barb, I notify you that I am already a pensiner. Here in SA we get only R400 a month therefore we live with difficulty. The money we get for pension is very very little to give us better living. Dear Barb, a thousand thanks for your kindness and apologizing for thus troubling you.*

Bye bye Barb. We wish God may bless you and your family now and ever. God may bless you always. Thank you dear, Ta-Ta. Yours in love, Elizabeth Mngadi

My suspicion and attention sharpened as I remembered Mozambican phrases and the ubiquitous "ta ta" everyone used there when parting. I also remembered how surprised I was when I first came to South Africa to find that no one ever used the phrase "ta ta." *But this letter was supposed to be from Elizabeth, who had never been to Mozambique.*

I explained to Barbara, who had never been there, why I thought the Mozambican name and sign-off were suspicious. Barbara thought for a moment.

"Betty, do you remember that man we met who was living with her back when we lunched together at her house? He was only about 35 years old. He couldn't be an old man now. He was a miner from Mozambique, remember?"

"I do. And she called him Jack, probably a nickname for Johannes. I wonder what happened to his wife in Mozambique. Anyway, I think her Jack, a clever and resourceful man as I remember, must still be living there!

We both sat quietly, thinking hard about this new information and the letter supposedly from Elizabeth. Slowly I said, "Barbara, I think this letter actually tells us that Elizabeth has joined her ancestors."

Barbara nodded sadly. We both sighed, mulling over our own thoughts, remembering Elizabeth in all her rotund glory and unquenchable spirit.

Finally, I looked again at Barbara and proposed, "Shall we have tea to honor Elizabeth, her life and the adventures we had thanks to her?"

I poured out our tea. Slowly we settled back with our teacups. I put in five spoonfuls of sugar, stirring vigorously, just as Elizabeth would have done.

ABOUT THE AUTHOR

Elizabeth Schneider lived in South Africa a total of fourteen years between 1975 and 1996, the period when apartheid-related violence escalated and Nelson Mandela became president after 27 years in prison. Concerned and curious about life for the black population, she determined to befriend her flat cleaner, Elizabeth Mngadi. *Forbidden Friends* is based on the author's detailed diary of their evolving relationship and their personal confrontations with apartheid.

A professional artist and photographer, she earned her Ph.D. in African Art at the University of Witwatersrand for *Paint, Pride and Politics*, a study of the distinctive wall paintings by Ndebele tribal women. The New York Public Library named her book, *The Ndebele,* "Best Book for the Teenage" in 1998.

Elizabeth Schneider currently lives in Northern California.

Made in the USA
San Bernardino, CA
17 June 2014